A CONCEPTUAL FRAMEWORK FOR EDUCATIONAL OBJECTIVES

A Holistic Approach to Traditional Taxonomies

A. Dean Hauenstein

University Press of America,® Inc.
Lanham • New York • Oxford

Copyright © 1998
University Press of America,® Inc.
4720 Boston Way
Lanham, Maryland 20706

12 Hid's Copse Rd.
Cummor Hill, Oxford OX2 9JJ

Library of Congress Cataloging-in-Publication Data

Hauenstein, A. Dean.
A new conceptual framework for educational objectives / A. Dean
Hauenstein.
p.   cm.
Includes bibliographical references and index.
1. Education—Aims and objectives. 2. Knowledge, Theory of. 3.
Learning, Psychology of. 4. Cognition. 5. Affect (Psychology) 6.
Perceptual—motor learning. 7. Child development. 8. Curriculum
planning. I. Title.
LB17.H39 1997   370'.1'2—dc21   98-44920 CIP

ISBN 0-7618-0994-5 (cloth: alk. ppr.)
ISBN 0-7618-0995-3 (pbk: alk. ppr.)

⊖™ The paper used in this publication meet the minimum
requirements of American National Standard for information
Sciences—Permanence of Paper for Printed Library Materials,
ANSI Z39.48—1984

Contents

iv

List of Tables

Chapter 6

List of Figures

Chapter 1
Chapter 2
Chapter 3
Chapter 4
Chapter 5
Chapter 6

Preface

The audiences for this book are elementary, middle school, secondary, vocational, technical, and adult teachers and curriculum planners. The book is intended as a supplemental textbook for individuals enrolled in graduate educational psychology courses, graduate seminars, and curriculum and methods courses in their areas of specialization that are concerned with educational objectives. It is also intended as a reference for inservice teacher training, updating, and development in school systems and organizations and agencies involved with training personnel.

The teacher's job is to prepare students for living a productive life in society. Students should be knowledgeable of the world around them, be acculturated to the society in which they live, and be competent to succeed in life. Students without a strong educational foundation will face hard economic and social obstacles in their future. Traditional approaches to education have not succeeded as well as desired. It is necessary to go back to basics--our educational objectives, and overhaul them in a way which will help teachers enable their students to gain a better education for life and work in society.

The purpose of this book is to provide teachers and curriculum planners with a holistic approach to traditional taxonomies of educational objectives. The holistic approach includes a conceptual framework for educational objectives and redefined cognitive, affective, and psychomotor domain taxonomies of objectives for whole learning. Traditional cognitive, affective, and psychomotor domains and their taxonomies of objectives are treated as separate and unconnected entities, are too numerous, often incompatible, and often too difficult to apply in the classroom. This book posits an instructional system which includes a composite fourth domain, a *behavioral domain*, as a means of consolidating and unifying the domains, reducing the number of taxonomic categories and subcategories, facilitating classroom application, and providing for the integration of subject matter from various disciplines, whether the redefined taxonomies are used separately or as a composite for teaching the whole individual.

This book supports some of the tenets of constructivism, such as: individuals construct their own knowledge from their experiences; individuals learn as whole persons; subject matter from various disciplines is interconnected; and that curriculum and instruction should be student-centered.

The conceptual framework is an instructional system with information/content (others' knowledge) as input for accommodating the interconnectedness of subject matter, process objectives (cognitive, affective, psychomotor, behavioral) for student-centered whole learning, and output (outcomes) as knowledgeable, acculturated, competent individuals. The outcomes are monitored and evaluated and necessary adjustments are fed back to the information inputs and process objectives.

The conceptual framework and redefined taxonomies are the result of a systematic analysis, evaluation, and redefinition of the cognitive, affective, and psychomotor taxonomies of educational objectives. These three taxonomies of objectives are synthesized into a *composite behavioral domain* with five categories of objectives. The behavioral domain taxonomy and instructional system provide the teacher a means to focus on student-centered understandings, skills, and dispositions, to more accurately classify levels of objectives, identify the learning/development levels of students, and develop appropriate objectives, lessons, and outcomes for students for whole learning.

This book critically examines the longstanding taxonomies of educational objectives, namely: Bloom et al. (1956) *Taxonomy of Educational Objectives: Cognitive Domain,* Krathwohl et al. (1964) *Taxonomy of Educational Objectives: Affective Domain,* and various Psychomotor Domains. Rules for taxonomic structuring are set forth as criteria to judge the validity of the taxonomies and serve as a basis for analyzing, qualifying, and redefining the taxonomies. Redefined cognitive, affective, and psychomotor domain taxonomies of objectives are synthesized into a unified behavioral domain.

It is taken as a fact that an individual learns as a whole person. A person does not have an intellectual experience without some feeling about it. A person does not do a task without some knowledge of how to do it and have a disposition, that what he/she does has some value. Our educational objectives should reflect the fact that each individual learns as a *whole person.*

If one were to count the traditional and most often cited cognitive, affective, and psychomotor objectives in the professional literature, one would find a total of 63 categories and subcategories of objectives. *The normal preservice or classroom teacher has difficulty applying and implementing these numerous classifications of objectives in teaching the whole individual.* This may be the reason many teachers focus primarily on the cognitive domain and often neglect the equally important affective and psychomotor domains or the individual as a whole person.

Chapter 1 introduces the context of constructivism, introduces the traditional taxonomies of educational objectives, briefly discusses the need to redefine and simplify the taxonomies of educational objectives, and provides a definition of terms. The conceptual framework (instructional system) is introduced with information/content (others' knowledge) as inputs, process as objectives, outcomes as outputs, and evaluation feedback as a means to adjust the inputs and objectives to maintain the outcomes at the desired performance level. A *behavioral* domain with five categories and fifteen subcategories of objectives is also introduced as a *composite* of the cognitive, affective, and psychomotor domains.

Chapter 2 defines *knowledge* and differentiates knowledge from *information and content.* Information/content is an input to the process objectives. Information/content (others' knowledge) is seen as an external input and does not become knowledge (internal) for the student until the student has had some experience with the information. Information/content (others' knowledge) is classified into four functions. These are: 1) symbolic information/content, i.e., *signs, symbols*--the language used to communicate all information and knowledge, 2) prescriptive information/content prescribes *what ought to be*, 3) descriptive information/content describes *what was, is, will be*, and 4) technological information/content is knowledge of *what to do* and knowledge gained by experience of *how to do it*. Symbolic information/ content is an input to the objectives of each domain. Symbolic and prescriptive information/content are essential inputs for the affective domain objectives. Symbolic and descriptive information/content are essential inputs for the cognitive domain objectives. Symbolic and technological information/content are essential inputs for the psychomotor domain objectives. All four are essential inputs to the behavioral domain. As per the tenets of constructivism, the conceptual framework provides for the integration of subject matter via the four categories of information/content inputs.

Chapter 3 redefines the cognitive domain categories of objectives in relation to five taxonomic criteria or rules. Each subordinate objective is critiqued against the criteria and a rationale for change is discussed. A redefined taxonomy of objectives is presented with definitions and applicable test descriptors. Symbolic and descriptive information/content (others' knowledge) are the primary information inputs to the cognitive domain.

Chapter 4 redefines the affective domain categories of objectives in relation to the five taxonomic criteria or rules. Each subordinate objective is critiqued against the criteria and a rationale for change is discussed. A redefined taxonomy of objectives is presented with definitions and applicable test descriptors. Symbolic and prescriptive information/content (others' knowledge) are the primary information inputs. Also included are suggestions for teachers for implementing this important, but often neglected domain.

Chapter 5 redefines the psychomotor domain categories of objectives in relation to the taxonomic criteria or rules. A redefined taxonomy of objectives is presented with definitions and applicable test descriptors. Symbolic and technological information/content (others' knowledge) are the primary information inputs. The influence of all three domains upon learning is discussed via a vector model. The theme of this section is *one behaves in accord with what one knows, can do, and how one feels about a situation.*

Chapter 6 integrates and defines the cognitive, affective, psychomotor domains as a unified *behavioral domain.* The behavioral domain taxonomy is presented as a learning process and provides teachers and curriculum planners with a means to identify a students' learning level. Assessment of student development and achievement is discussed via a behavioral profile. The behavioral domain objectives are classified as short term and long term objectives for classroom application. How to write objectives for the behavioral domain is also indicated. The 63 traditional categories and subcategories of objectives are synthesized and reduced to *five generic categories and fifteen subcategories of educational objectives.*

All of the taxonomies, (cognitive, affective, psychomotor, and behavioral) have five levels of development and difficulty with levels compatible to each other in purpose and function. The end result is that teachers and curriculum planners will have a better understanding of the learning process, be able to classify their objectives accurately, be more cognizant of student learning levels, and be better equipped to provide appropriate interconnected subject matter, objectives, and lessons for their students.

Acknowledgments

I am grateful to my colleagues who reviewed the manuscript during its development. I wish to thank: Francis DiVesta, Pennsylvania State University; Martin Hamburger, New York University; and Robert Farrell, and Robert Vos of Florida International University for their review in the early stages of development of this book. I wish to express my appreciation to Charles Divita, Jr., Erskine S. Dottin, Stephen M. Fain, and Colleen A. Ryan, of Florida International University for their critiques during the latter stages of the book. I also wish to express my appreciation for the graduate students in my curriculum classes who served as sounding boards in the development of these materials.

Chapter 1

The Conceptual Framework

Introduction

It is taken as a fact that individuals learn as *whole persons*. They use their feelings, their brains, and their bodies in the learning process. Simply put, they have feelings prior to a learning situation, they use their senses to receive information, their intellect to process information/content into understandings, their muscles to perform necessary actions, and the effects of which, in turn, influence their feelings about the experience. This process is repeated during a learning situation and occurs whenever new information/content is encountered. Continual repetition of this cycle, with new information/content input, provides the process for individuals to learn and develop their understandings, skills, and dispositions. The result of the learning process is that, when a situation is encountered, individuals behave in accord with what they know, can do, and how they feel about it.

On the one hand, learning engages the whole individual. On the other hand, we have educational objectives that are separated into cognitive, affective, and psychomotor domains. The cognitive domain deals with the process of knowing and the development of intellectual abilities and skills. The affective domain deals with influences of feelings, values, and beliefs on one's behavior. The psychomotor domain deals with developing physical actions, abilities and skills. To date, there has been no attempt to synthesize or consolidate the three domains to parallel or engage the whole individual in the learning process.

Constructivism is a current theme in professional education. Constructivism is based on assumptions that learners do not passively acquire knowledge but construct their knowledge based on their experiences. Their knowledge changes as they use and test their knowledge in new experiences. Content or subject matter is viewed as interconnected concepts rather than fragmented facts, and the curriculum is student-centered as opposed to teacher-centered. These ideas are facilitated by the conceptual framework (instructional system) and redefined taxonomies in this book.

Any system has components of inputs, processes, outputs, and feedback. The conceptual framework (instructional system) has information/content as inputs, objectives and their inherent learning experiences as process, outcomes (achievements) as outputs, and feedback for adjusting the system. To facilitate the conceptual framework, models, criteria, and rationales are presented and redefinition of the taxonomies are made accordingly. Redefined cognitive, affective, and psychomotor domains and their taxonomies simplify and facilitate compatibility in levels of objectives across the three separate domains. The conceptual framework is applicable to the cognitive, affective, and psychomotor objectives whether they are *used separately* or as a *composite behavioral domain*.

Definitions

The terms encountered in this chapter may be new to many readers. Dealing with the terminology and distinctions between the cognitive, affective, psychomotor, and behavioral domains and their categories and subcategories of objectives is complex and requires careful reading. The following definitions are presented to facilitate understanding of the terms and basic ideas presented herein.

Domain--a distinctly delimited sphere of knowledge or of intellectual activity. In this book, the domains are posited as the cognitive domain (the process of knowing and development of intellectual abilities and skills), the affective domain (the development of dispositions, i.e., prevailing tendencies related to feelings, values, and beliefs), the psychomotor domain (development of physical abilities and skills), and the behavioral domain (development of knowledgeable, acculturated, competent individuals).

Taxonomy--a classification system that establishes the hierarchy of the parts to the whole. An orderly classification of items according to their presumed relationship. A hierarchy presumes that a lower order class is a prerequisite to a higher order class. Also, in a hierarchy, a higher order class incorporates more specific lower order classes. In this book, taxonomies of educational objectives in the cognitive, affective, psychomotor, and behavioral domains, are categorized in an order of learning, development, and complexity.

Category--a class, group or classification of any kind. In this book, the domains are divided into categories and subcategories in accord with a set of taxonomic rules and coded to reflect their order (or level) in a hierarchy, e.g., 1.0, 2.0, 3.0. Subcategories are also coded in relation to their place in the hierarchy, e.g., category 1.0 may have subcategories coded 1.1, 1.2, 1.3, and category 2.0 may have subcategories coded 2.1, 2.2, etc.

Information/Content--from the students point of view, it is others' knowledge of subjects and topics as found in books, charts, films, computer networks, etc., and people, *other than themselves*. It is the information/content input for the individual's acquisition of the subject matter.

Objective--something toward which an effort is directed, an end of action, a goal. In this book, a category of objectives indicates a *level of development and/or achievement*. For example, in the redefined cognitive domain, the taxonomic categories are: conceptualization, comprehension, application, evaluation, and synthesis, which represent generic *levels* of intellectual abilities and skills. Conceptualization is a prerequisite to comprehension, comprehension is a prerequisite to application, application is a prerequisite to evaluation, etc. Specific objectives vary with the information/content inputs selected, the learning level of the student, and related learning experiences. A specific objective specifies: 1) conditions, i.e., content and manner of input, e.g., after watching a film demonstrating linear metric measurement; 2) a terminal behavior, e.g., measure and record the linear dimensions of various objects; and 3) a criterion indicating an acceptable level of performance, e.g., to within plus or minus one millimeter.

Cognitive--the act or process of knowing in the broadest sense, an intellectual process by which knowledge is gained about perceptions or ideas. In this book, it is that domain of knowledge involved with the process of knowing and development of intellectual abilities and skills.

Affective--influence on conduct of an individual, applies to a stimulus strong enough to bring about a reaction, or bring about some modification, without total change of the individual. In this book, it is that domain of knowledge involved with developing dispositions (prevailing tendencies) in relation to feelings, values, and beliefs.

Psychomotor--muscular/physical action believed to *ensue from prior conscious mental activity*. In this book, it is that domain of knowledge involved with developing physical abilities and skills following an input of information/content.

Behavioral--the manner in which a person behaves in reacting to a social stimulus, or to inner need or to a combination thereof. Observable activity, measurable in terms of quantifiable effects on the individual whether rising from internal or external stimulus. Any thing that a person does that involves action and response to stimulation. In this book, it is that domain of knowledge involved with developing knowledgeable, acculturated, and competent individuals.

Knowledge--the fact or condition of knowing, the fact or condition of

Table 1A
Comparison of Traditional Taxonomies of Educational Objectives

	Lowest 1.00	2.00	3.00	4.00	Levels 5.00	6.00	Highest 7.00
Cognitive Domain Categories (Bloom et al. 1956)	Knowledge	Comprehension	Application	Analysis	Synthesis	Evaluation	
Affective Domain Categories (Krathwohl et al. 1964)	Receiving	Responding	Valuing	Organization	Characterization		
Psychomotor Domain Categories							
(Simpson 1966)	Perception	Set	Guided response	Mechanism	Complex overt response	Adaptation	Origination
(Dave 1970)	Imitation	Manipulation	Precision	Articulation	Naturalization		
(Harrow 1972)	Familiarization	Fundamentals	Development	Adjusting & adapting	Perfection & maintenance		
(Hauenstein 1972)	Perceiving	Imitating	Manipulating	Performing	Perfecting		

knowing with a considerable degree of familiarity gained through experience. Acquaintance with a theoretical or practical understanding of some branch of science, art, learning or other area involving study, research or practice and the acquisition of skills. In this book, knowledge is internal and intrinsic to the learner and is what is known after some experience with an input of information/content.

Disposition--a prevailing tendency, inclination, a natural attitude toward things. The tendency to act in a certain manner under given circumstances, a demeanor, customary mood and attitude toward the life around one. In this book, dispositions refer to prevailing tendencies and their modification.

Traditional Taxonomies of Educational Objectives

The most widely accepted taxonomies of educational objectives in the professional literature are the *Taxonomy of Educational Objectives, The Classification of Educational Goals, Handbook I: Cognitive Domain* (Bloom, et al., 1956), and the *Taxonomy of Educational Objectives, The Classification of Educational Goals, Handbook II: Affective Domain* (Krathwohl, Bloom, and Masia 1964) and *The Classification of Educational Objectives, Psychomotor Domain* (Simpson 1966). The taxonomies are arranged in a hierarchy by levels of presumed development and difficulty. There is no composite behavioral domain to facilitate the attainment of objectives for the development of the *whole individual*.

Traditional taxonomies of the cognitive, affective, and psychomotor domains are treated as separate entities in the professional literature. As separate entities, they lack a unifying context, have different numbers of categories, are unparallel in categorical intent, within and across categories and subcategories, and vary in the expression of terms.

The *major* categories of traditional cognitive, affective, and psychomotor taxonomies are presented in Table 1A: Comparison of Traditional Taxonomies of Educational Objectives for comparative purposes. It shows the names of the *major* categories and the differences in the numbers and levels of the major categories. In the late 1960's and early 1970's, four psychomotor domains appeared in the professional literature. These are also included in Table 1A.

The cognitive domain has six major categories of objectives. The affective

Note

For the reader unfamiliar with taxonomies, a condensed version of the cognitive domain is shown in Appendix A. A condensed version of the affective domain objectives is shown in Appendix B. Table 1A shows the major categories and levels of the psychomotor, cognitive, and affective domains.

domain has five major categories. The psychomotor domains range from five to seven major categories for a total of 18 major categories of objectives. Table 2B: Traditional Domains and Categories, summarizes the disparity and incompatibility of the number and level of categories *and subcategories* in the three domains. *The normal classroom teacher has difficulty applying these numerous (63) categories and subcategories of objectives* in teaching the individual. There is a need to redefine, simplify, make compatible, and reduce the number of objectives.

It would be useful to have a synthesized taxonomy with, for example, five categories, that reflects a composite of the cognitive, affective, and psychomotor domain objectives. Such a taxonomy would provide the teacher a means to more accurately classify the level of objectives they write, the learning/development level of students, and develop appropriate curriculum and specific objectives and outcome measurements. To remedy this situation, a conceptual framework (instructional system) is posited herein as a unifying context. The cognitive, affective, and psychomotor objectives of each domain are redefined in this book and reduced to five categories each, and they are combined into a new composite behavioral domain with five categories and fifteen subcategories (three subcategories for each category). See Table 1B: Traditional Domains and Categories: Behavioral (synthesized composite).

Table 1B
Traditional Domains and Categories

Domains	Categories	Subcategories
Cognitive (Bloom, et al. 1956)	6	23
Affective (Krathwohl, et al. 1964)	5	13
Psychomotor (Simpson, 1966)	7	8
Totals	**18**	**44**
Grand Total = **63** categories and subcategories		
- -		
Behavioral (synthesized composite)	**5**	**15**
Grand Total = **20** categories and subcategories		

Conceptual Framework

A system involves the interaction of its components: inputs, process,

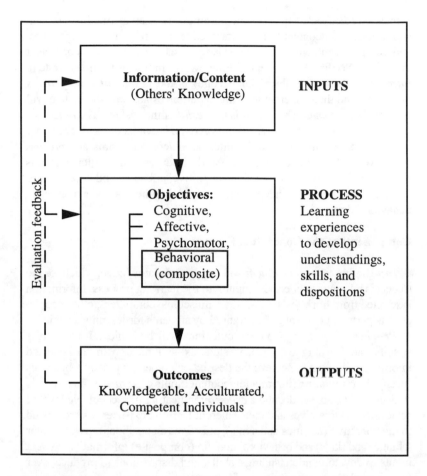

Fig. 1.1 Conceptual Framework

Fig. 1.1 shows a system for instruction with information/content (others' knowledge) as inputs to the cognitive, affective, psychomotor, and behavioral (composite) process objectives (learning experiences) to develop understandings, skills, and dispositions to produce outcomes of knowledgeable, acculturated, competent individuals. Evaluation feedback provides for adjustment of the information/content inputs and process objectives to maintain outcomes at the desired performance level.

outputs, and feedback. The conceptual framework is an instructional system with information/content (others' knowledge) as input, process objectives, and output (outcomes) as knowledgeable, acculturated, competent individuals. See Fig. 1.1 Conceptual Framework. In the instructional system, *information/content* (others' knowledge) is the key *input*. The *process objectives* and their inherent learning experiences are how the system will *achieve the outcomes*. The *output* is the *result* of the system. The *outcomes* of the process objectives are monitored and evaluated and necessary *adjustments*, are *fed back* to the information/content inputs and process objectives to keep the outcomes at the desired performance level. In this conceptual framework, the redefined cognitive, affective, and psychomotor domains can be used independently of each other or as a combined behavioral domain.

Components of the Conceptual Framework

Inputs: Information/Content--other people's knowledge, which for the student is information or content input into the learning process. Information is selected from libraries, books, films, museums, computers, other people, etc., as pertinent content to be acquired by students for learning a subject.

Process: Objectives--how the outcomes will be achieved. Objectives specify the learning experiences students will have with the selected information/content to achieve the desired outcomes. Typically, objectives specify the *conditions* (information/content inputs), the *tasks* (or activities) students will be able to do, and a *criterion* indicating the acceptable level of achievement. Objectives and their inherent learning experiences are related to the cognitive (abilities and skills), affective (dispositions), psychomotor (abilities and skills) and behavioral domain (composite) information/content inputs to develop understandings, skills, and dispositions to produce, over time, knowledgeable, acculturated, competent individuals.

Outputs: Outcomes--the results, the change in behavior or level of achievement resulting from the inputs, objectives, and learning experiences. *Outcomes may be determined and measured for any category performance level*, e.g., cognitive domain: comprehension level, or affective domain: valuing level, or psychomotor domain: simulation level.

Evaluation feedback: *Adjustments*--the needed changes in the information/content and process objectives to maintain the outcomes at a desired performance level. Outcomes are monitored and differences between the expected and actual level of achievement are determined and adjustments are made in the information/content and/or the objectives.

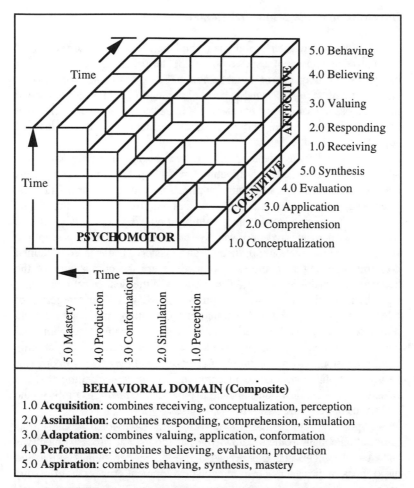

BEHAVIORAL DOMAIN (Composite)

1.0 **Acquisition**: combines receiving, conceptualization, perception
2.0 **Assimilation**: combines responding, comprehension, simulation
3.0 **Adaptation**: combines valuing, application, conformation
4.0 **Performance**: combines believing, evaluation, production
5.0 **Aspiration**: combines behaving, synthesis, mastery

Fig. 1.2. Components of the Behavioral Domain

Fig. 1.2 shows the building blocks of the behavioral domain. The behavioral domain is a composite of redefined cognitive, affective, and psychomotor domains. All three domains are essential for each block and level for *whole learning.* Higher level categories include all of the prerequisite lower levels, e.g., a 3.0 level objective includes all of the 1.0 and 2.0 components in each domain. The time required to develop understandings, skills, and dispositions is cumulative. Lower levels require more time because of the number of components.

Introduction to the Behavioral Domain

In the following chapters, the domains and their taxonomies are redefined to: 1) provide consistent expression of the terms, i.e., all terms denoting categories and subcategories must be able to be expressed as gerund nouns (words ending in *ing*), 2) enable parallel compatibility of terminology and intent across the same level of categories in each of the domains, 3) reflect the instructional system, and 4) reduce the number of categories and subcategories of objectives.

Also in the following chapters, the traditional cognitive domain objectives are critically analyzed and redefined with five taxonomic categories: conceptualization, comprehension, application, evaluation, and synthesis. The affective domain is critically analyzed and redefined with five taxonomic categories: receiving, responding, valuing, believing, and behaving. The psychomotor domain is redefined with five taxonomic categories: perception, simulation, conformation, production, and mastery. These three redefined domains and their taxonomies of objectives are the components of the behavioral domain. See Fig. 1.2 Components of the Behavioral Domain.

A behavioral (composite) domain is defined with five categories of objectives as: acquisition, assimilation, adaptation, performance, and aspiration. *Acquisition* combines the categories of receiving, perception, and conceptualization. *Assimilation* combines the categories of responding, comprehension, and simulation. *Adaptation* combines the categories of valuing, application, and conformation. *Performance* combines the categories of believing, evaluation, and production. *Aspiration* combines the categories of behaving, synthesis, and mastery.

As per the conceptual framework, the *behavioral* domain has information/content (others' knowledge) as inputs. The process objectives and their inherent learning experiences to develop understandings, skills, and dispositions are posited as a learning and development process. In brief, this process is: *acquisition*--the gaining of new information/content, *assimilation*--working the new knowledge into what is already known, *adaptation*--applying what is known to various situations or problems in relation to one's skills and values, *performance*--producing as a matter of routine and accommodating new knowledge, skills, and values, and *aspiration*-- seeking to do better, to excel, in accord with one's beliefs and skills. The outcome is seen as a knowledgeable, acculturated, competent individual. Evaluation of the outcomes is fed back to the information/content inputs and process objectives for adjustments to maintain the desired outcome performance level.

Since the behavioral domain is a composite of the cognitive, affective, and psychomotor domains, it needs to be visualized as a holistic entity with interrelated components. The components of the behavioral domain can be visualized as building blocks of a truncated cube. The foundational layer contains more building blocks than the next layer of blocks, and so forth, until the highest level is achieved. Similarly, the time required to develop understandings, skills, and dispositions is greater at the foundational layer because there are many more blocks. The time required to develop higher levels of development is cumulative with each block and layer adding to the time required for learning, development, and achievement. See Fig. 1.2 Components of the Behavioral Domain.

In the next chapter, knowledge is defined and classified into four categories as information/content inputs applicable to each of the domains. In Chapters 3, 4, and 5, a set of taxonomic rule are established as criteria for analyzing and evaluating the traditional taxonomies. Each of the traditional taxonomies are critically examined in relation to the criteria. Deficiencies and discrepancies are identified and appropriate changes are made in terminology, hierarchical order, and reduction of numbers of categories as applicable to the taxonomies. Chapter 6 defines and presents the taxonomy of objectives of the composite behavioral domain.

Summary

It is taken as a fact, that individuals learn as whole persons. Traditional taxonomies of the cognitive, affective, psychomotor domains are treated as separate entities, lacking a unifying context. Traditional taxonomies are inconsistent and incompatible in terminology, are unparallel in the numbers of levels of categories, and are too numerous for practical classroom application. Tables are presented to show the diversity of terminology and numbers of categories of traditional taxonomies of educational objectives.

Terms such as: domain, taxonomy, category, information/content, objective, cognitive, affective, psychomotor, behavioral, knowledge, and dispositions are introduced and defined to facilitate understanding of the concepts.

A conceptual framework (instructional system) is introduced. The instructional system has components of: information/content inputs; process objectives and their inherent learning experiences to develop understandings, skills, and dispositions; outputs/outcomes as knowledgeable, acculturated, competent individuals; and evaluation feedback for adjusting the system to maintain the outcomes at the desired performance level.

The behavioral domain is introduced and is composed of redefined components of the cognitive, affective, and psychomotor domains. The following chapters deal with defining knowledge, and redefining the cognitive, affective, and psychomotor domains and their taxonomies, and defining a new behavioral domain in accord with the conceptual framework.

Questions to Consider

1.   What is the purpose of the conceptual framework?
2.   How does the instructional system work? What are the components?
3.   What implications might the conceptual framework have for current practice in using cognitive, affective, and psychomotor objectives?
4.   Do you agree or disagree there are too many categories of educational objectives? Why?
5.   Do you think there is compatibility of terminology among the major categories of cognitive, affective, and psychomotor domains? See Table 1A.
6.   Is there a difference between information and knowledge?
7.   Why is information considered to be others' knowledge?
8.   How does the conceptual framework reflect the ideas of constructivism?
9.   What questions do you have?

References

1.   Bloom, Benjamin. S. (Ed.), Englehart, Max. D., Furst, Edward. J., Hill, Walker H. and Krathwohl, David R., 1956. *Taxonomy of educational objectives. The classification of educational goals, Handbook I: Cognitive domain.* New York: Longmans, Green, Co.
2.   Dave, R. H. as reported in Robert J. Armstrong, et. al, 1970. *Developing and writing behavioral objectives.* Tucson, Arizona: Innovators Press.
3.   Harrow, Anita. 1972. *Taxonomy of the psychomotor domain: A guide for developing behavioral objectives.* New York: David McKay Co. Inc.
4.   Hauenstein, A. Dean, 1972. *Curriculum planning for behavioral development.* Worthington, Ohio: Charles A. Jones Publishing Company.
5.   Krathwohl, David R., Bloom, Benjamin S., and Masia, Bertram B. 1964. *Taxonomy of educational objectives. The classification of educational goals, Handbook II: Affective domain.* New York: David McKay Co. Inc.
6.   Simpson, B. J. 1966. *The classification of educational objectives, psychomotor domain.* Illinois Teacher of Home Economics, vol. X, no. 4.

Chapter 2

Knowledge: Defined

Introduction

Chapter 1 presented Table 1A: Comparison of Traditional Taxonomies of Educational Objectives. As one can see from Table 1A, *Knowledge* is the first category in Bloom's et al. taxonomy of cognitive objectives and is the foundation of and is prerequisite to the higher level categories. It may be useful to briefly examine what *knowledge* represents and what its characteristics are.

Knowledge is the foundation of the educational system. However, it is an error to believe that whatever is transmitted by teachers in the classroom is knowledge. What is being transmitted is the teacher's knowledge, (or someone else's knowledge), *which for the student is information.* Information/content does not become knowledge for the student until the student has had some experience with the information/content. From the student's point of view, what is normally called knowledge is really someone else's knowledge. Information/content (other people's knowledge) is an input and does not become the student's knowledge until it has been conceptualized and understood. This information/content may be input in the form of books, media, computers, lectures, demonstrations, and such.

There are numerous sources of information/content. These sources range from what is found in the libraries of the world, to the internet, museums, films, and the knowledge of each individual. Teachers have these and other sources to draw upon to provide information/content to students. From these sources, teachers select content applicable to the subject they teach. However, there is no assurance that students will be exposed to an adequate range of information/content to become fully knowledgeable about the subject.

Assurance can be provided if teachers use a simple classification scheme to ensure that input of selected information/content encompasses all aspects of the subject. For example, students should be familiar with the common and technical language of the subject, e.g., vocabulary, formulae, symbols,

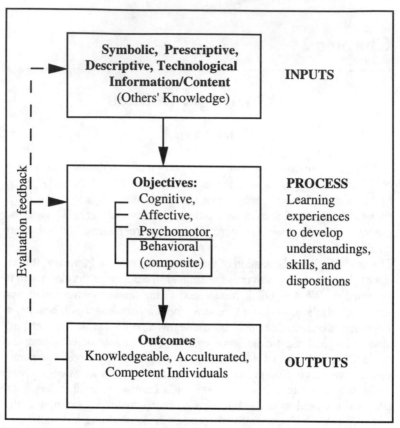

Fig. 2.1 Conceptual Framework

Fig. 2.1 shows a system for instruction with symbolic, prescriptive, descriptive, and technological information/content (others' knowledge) as inputs to the cognitive, affective, psychomotor, and behavioral (composite) process objectives (learning experiences) to develop understandings, skills, and dispositions to produce knowledgeable, acculturated, competent individuals. Evaluation feedback provides for adjustment of the information/content inputs and process objectives to maintain outcomes at the desired performance level.

and concepts. This input is termed *symbolic* information/content. Students should also get the why's and wherefore's of the subject, e.g., the values, worthwhileness, and beliefs associated with the subject. This input is termed *prescriptive* information/content. They should also be exposed to the pertinent facts available in current literature or research. This input is termed *descriptive* information/content. They should also have access to the knowledge of what to do and the doing related to the subject. These inputs are termed *technological* information/content. See Fig. 2.1 Conceptual Framework. These four classifications of information/content (others' knowledge) as inputs in the learning process are described further as follows.

Classification of Information/Content Inputs by Function

Holistically, all types of knowledge can be classified under one of the four categories: formal, prescriptive, descriptive, and technological (Towers, Lux, and Ray, 1966). In this book *symbolic* replaces *formal* as it is more descriptive of the classification. It is logical that all four categories must be present for a well-rounded education. The function of each category of information/content is summarized as follows. It should be understood that, in relation to the student, *all forms of information/content inputs are other people's knowledge and are external.* After a student has a learning experience with the information/content, it then becomes knowledge for the student. The treatment of knowledge as an input is examined further in Chapter 3, The Cognitive Domain: Redefined.

Symbolic Information/Content Inputs

Symbolic information/content inputs are conceptual sign and symbol tools applicable to all information and knowledge. Symbolic information/content provides the meaningful sets of signs and symbols for communicating all concepts and ideas. All forms and categories of knowledge rely upon signs, symbols and concepts for conveying information/content; therefore, all information/content contain symbolic knowledge. Linguistics, mathematics, chemistry, art, graphics, music, theater, literature, and physics are examples of subjects in which signs and symbols function as *representations of ideas and concepts for communication purposes.* Any written word, spoken word, sound, form, touch, smell, taste, etc., expressed in signs and symbols that can be interpreted as having meaning, constitute symbolic knowledge. The function of symbolic information/content is to establish the encoding and decoding (expression and interpretation) of terms and meanings. For example the alphabetic and numeric symbols in a sentence facilitate the interpretation of the meaning. Symbolic information/content can be recognized by meaningful signs, symbols, vocabulary, nomenclature, and particularly, by its organization. (Hauenstein 1971, 11).

Prescriptive Information/Content Inputs

Prescriptive information/content inputs are concepts and ideas which function as the embodiment of *what ought to be*. Prescriptive information/content embodies values and beliefs of what ought to be good, bad, beautiful, ugly, right, wrong, pleasure, pain, true, false, happiness, sadness, etc., or anywhere between the extremes. Prescriptive inputs are speculations found largely in philosophy, logic, morals, ethics, theology, law, and the like. According to Maccia (1965), these speculations may be about forms, events, values, or practices. Form speculations are concerned with structures. Event speculations are concerned with occurrences. Value speculations are concerned with worthwhileness. Practice speculations are concerned with methodology (Maccia 1965, 4-5).

Descriptive Information/Content Inputs

Descriptive information/content inputs are concepts and ideas that express available knowledge about a phenomenon (an observable fact or event) and its relationships. This knowledge may increase or decrease the probability that something is a fact. Facts are established by observing the frequency and consistency of occurrence of phenomena. Since descriptive concepts are the embodiments of *what was, is,* and *will be*, they are common to the physical, biological, and social sciences. Physics, chemistry, and biology are concerned with *what is*. Archaeology and history are concerned with *what was*. Projections or predictions extrapolated from data are concerned with *what will be*.

Technological Information/Content Inputs

Technological information/content are those *knowledges and abilities that seek to increase the efficiency and effectiveness of human behavior. They include the knowledge of and use of tools, materials, and processes in specific contexts*. Technological information/content includes those practices (actual performances or applications) found to be efficient and effective through experience. These best practices seek to establish the efficiency of event sequence or planned order of action to attain what is valued. Practices in which common technological knowledge is found, for example, include law, medicine, teaching, carpentry, piloting aircraft, and all other applied skills and knowledge. Technological knowledge and best practices are gained by the practical experience of doing it. For example, you can read and talk about how to fly an airplane all you want, but you do not really know how to fly until you have flown an airplane yourself.

Technological information/content deals with knowing *what to do and how to behave efficiently to bring about what is desired.* They require a clinical or practical experience to establish the effectiveness of the behavior and the usefulness of the knowledge. A noun ending in *ing* (gerund noun) is a good indicator of technological or doing or behaving knowledge. Everything that humankind has done, is doing, or will do, has a technology, but all technologies have not been well defined, codified or emphasized in the schools. Agriculture is a science whereas farming is a technology. Dentistry is a profession whereas brushing your teeth is a technology. The family is an institution whereas parenting is a technology. Education is an institution whereas teaching and learning are technologies. Everything people do or engage in is made up of specific observable actions. These actions and processes (sequenced actions) are technologies and these technologies arc used to achieve some valued objective.

Technology and Behavior

One definition of technology is *the science of the application of knowledge to practical purposes.* The term *technology* is used in everyday language and is part of the common vocabulary. However, technology, is a term that is loosely used. To many people, technology means sophisticated mechanisms, computers, or hardware. This is a misnomer. It must be pointed out that *people develop and use techniques. Objects do not have techniques.* Hardware is the result or product of technology. People design, engineer, and produce products. The product, in turn, operates only as it was designed, engineered and manufactured to operate, no more and no less. The inanimate object has no inherent techniques of its own, not even a *high tech* computer. It is only through the application of knowledge for practical purposes that the computer exists. Thus, technologies are *process knowledge and actions,* which may include the knowledgeable and efficient use of tools, materials, and equipment to bring about what is valued. (Towers, Lux, and Ray 1996, 8-10). *Technology can be thought of as headware and handware to bring about what is valued.* The research project Technology for All Americans (1997), defines technology as human innovation in action. This involves the generation of knowledge and processes to develop systems that solve problems and extend human capabilities.

Technology is defined in this book as: *the knowledge of and the use of values, abilities, and skills to satisfy human wants and needs*. Technologies involve knowing what to do and the application of knowledge, values, actions, skills, abilities, tools, materials, and processes to accomplish a desired end. For a behavior to be a technology, it must be able to be *replicated* or reproduced. The uses of or applications of techniques are forms of behavior and conduct. Thus, everything that a person or a group does in a replicated manner to achieve an objective becomes a technology.

Some behaviors are more efficient and effective behaviors than others. Some relatively simple behaviors are low level technologies, while others are more complex and high level technologies. Brushing your teeth is a low level technology. Even so, some of us are not very good at it. Manufacturing an automobile is a high level technology. Cooking a meal is a technology. Parenting is a technology. Learning is a technology. Teaching is a technology. There is a body of knowledge that is learned and made more effective and efficient through doing, practice, and experience. For example, teacher education institutions rely heavily on *practice* or a period of *student teaching*. In fact, student teaching is consistently rated by students as the most significant learning experience in professional education. Similarly, medicine, law, dentistry, carpentry, and other disciplines have internships and apprenticeships in which essential and required knowledge of practice is gained before full licensure is granted. Method courses taken prior to internships attempt to provide the *knowledge of practice*. However, it must be recognized that it is in the *practice* that the knowledge of practice and the knowledge gained through doing are knit together to allow one to conduct one's behavior in a more effective and efficient manner.

Schools exist to transmit information (others' knowledge) and provide activities meaningfully to students, but information keeps changing and multiplying. It is next to impossible for teachers to keep abreast of their field, and keep the school curriculum and curriculum materials up-to-date. Teachers have been teaching their knowledge disciplines to students, or more accurately, passing on the information. They have been passing on information to students rather than teaching students to use information procedurally to improve their lives. For example, the focus of secondary school curriculum is primarily on disciplines or subjects such as: English, mathematics, algebra, geometry, trigonometry, calculus, biology, earth science, physics, chemistry, social science, music, art, history, Spanish, etc.

All of these subjects include information about phenomena and data, not behavior. The teacher and the student are left with the question of how to make the subject practical and relevant to life.

To be practical, to be educated, to be able to apply knowledge in the real world in which people live, implies, if not demands, that a school's curriculum be structured from a technological (behavioral) knowledge base. It is in the realm of the knowledge of practice that the application of knowledge is founded and demonstrated. Thus, to develop a relevant, practical, effective and efficient curriculum, the planners and teachers must work from a technological or behavioral base.

Teachers work with behavioral objectives most of the time. However, the behaviors are usually arbitrarily selected to fit or match some piece of symbolic, prescriptive, descriptive, or technological information of the subject rather than vice versa. It makes sense to first codify behaviors (practices or actions) drawn from the real world and then identify what students need to know to be able to perform. Such a structured *body of information/content (others' knowledge)* provides a broad conceptual map for making rational curricular decisions for instruction and learning. When information is organized or assembled *without* defining what students should be able to do (supported by what they should know), educational monsters are created and fall short of achieving goals. Curriculum planners are engaged in *educational alchemy* in hopes that their curriculum will prepare students for productive life and work in society.

Knowledge (Truth) Continuums

Truth has a range of definition. For purposes of this book, truth is the degree of confidence or trust one has that something is so. What is truth for one person may not be truth for another. However, the characteristic derivation of knowledge from truth can be identified. For example, *symbolic and prescriptive knowledge* (truths) is derived from and established by *consensus*. This can be called *analytic* knowledge (truths), because to establish what is accepted and valued as good, worthwhile, or valid requires analysis of the values, beliefs, and preferences held by a society, group, or person. *Descriptive and technological knowledge* (truths) is derived and established by *observation*. This can be called *experiential* knowledge because it requires repeated observations of real experiences to identify and establish truth. See Fig. 2.2 Derivation of Knowledge (Truths).

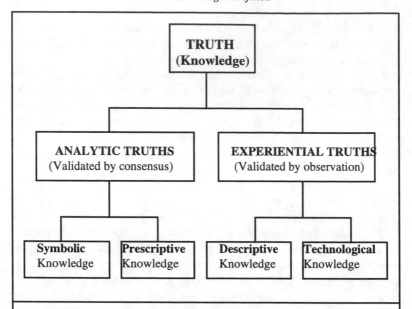

Symbolic knowledge (truths): *established by consensus, agreement. Sign and symbol tools of communications for all other knowledges.*
Examples: sciences, languages, mathematics, chemistry, graphics, art, musics, theater, literature, physics, drawing.

Prescriptive knowledge (truths): *established by consensus, agreement. Prescribes what ought to be. Speculations as to values, worthwhileness, structure, and occurances.*
Examples: philosophy, law, logic, ethics, morals, theology.

Descriptive knowledge (truths): *established by observations of the status, frequency, and probability of events and occurances. Describes what is, was, will be.*
Examples: algebra, geometry, history, archaeology, physics, chemistry.

Technological knowledge (truths): *established by knowledge of practice and experience. How to efficiently behave to bring about what is valued.*
Examples: engineering, medicine, farming, teaching, marketing, accounting.

Fig. 2.2 Derivation of Knowledge

Symbolic Knowledge (Truth) Continuum.

In the symbolic knowledge domain, what a sign, symbol or word means is only valid as long as people agree that it has a certain meaning and is consistent in their usage of the term. If, for example, we all agree to hereafter call a chair a *cham,* the word *cham* will convey the concept of the chair. There are swivel chams, rocking chams, reclining chams, desk chams, easy chams, etc. The symbolic word *cham* becomes the object we use to sit upon, a seat with legs or some other form for support. Likewise, words for concepts can be invented, be agreed upon, and become part of the symbolic knowledge structure if they are used consistently. For example, there seems to be no word to indicate what is inbetween micro and macro. We may invent the word *miacro* to indicate the middle range between the two extremes. However, it will only become part of the symbolic knowledge domain if people agree upon its meaning and refer to it consistently. Thus, if agreed, something may be referenced to the *miacro* level rather than the macro or micro level. Similarly, the term *chunnel* was evolved to designate the tunnel under the English channel connecting England to Europe.

Symbolic knowledge or truth can be placed on a continuum ranging from one extreme where there is no agreement, acceptance, or consensus to the other extreme where there is complete or a high degree of agreement, acceptance, and consensus. See Table 2A: Symbolic Knowledge (Truth) Continuum.

Table 2A
Symbolic Knowledge (Truth) Continuum (Validated by Consensus)

Is the truth (consensus, communication) established?

NO <---> YES

No acceptance,	High acceptance,
agreement, consensus.	agreement, consensus.
No communication.	High communication.

Prescriptive Knowledge (Truth) Continuum

Prescriptive knowledge is a value concept that relates to and may range between the extremes of good and evil, right and wrong, etc. These values and beliefs are established by consensus. They may be good or bad, right or wrong so long as people believe and agree on it. For example, we believe and agree in America that democracy is a better form of government than dictatorship, that democratic actions are preferable to undemocratic actions. We believe and agree that it is wrong to steal, rape, murder, etc., and we set penalties by law to enforce these tenets. We agree that discriminatory practices are detrimental to the common good and establish civil rights legislation to guard against them. However, it was not too long ago (1960's) that there was no general consensus. In another example, determining what is beautiful may be difficult. Beauty is in the eye of the beholder, as the saying goes. What is beautiful for one may not be so for another.

Prescriptive knowledge, those preferences, values, and beliefs, of *what ought to be* can be viewed on a continuum of pain to pleasure. Psychologists tell us that people are pleasure seeking rather than pain seeking. People move toward what is more pleasurable, more satisfying, more gratifying, useful, right, good, valued, and away from the opposites. People are willing to expose themselves to some *pain* if the experience will result in a greater good or an esteemed value. For example, war heroes are recognized for their valor because they were willing to place their lives in jeopardy (danger) to save the lives of others (greater good). Graduate students are willing to undergo the effort and work of study (some pain) in the expectation that they will benefit (some satisfaction) from the experience. The desired value may be a degree, higher pay, learning, or some other personal value. See Table 2B: Prescriptive Knowledge (Truth) Continuum.

Table 2B
Prescriptive Knowledge (Truth) Continuum (Validated by Consensus)

Is the truth (agreement on what ought to be) established?

PAIN <--> PLEASURE		
Evil	*Examples*	Good
Ugly		Beautiful
Wrong		Right
Authoritarian		Democratic
False		True
Unemployed		Employed
Immoral		Moral
Sad		Happy
Unlawful		Lawful

Descriptive Knowledge (Truth) Continuum

Descriptive knowledge such as that contained in the sciences establishes facts based on repeated observations of occurrences and phenomena. To be more accurate, scientists establish the probability that something is a fact based on the frequency and consistency (reliability) of the occurrences and phenomena. At one time, it was an accepted fact that the earth was the center of the solar system. This theory was demolished when Copernicus, in 1473, observed that the earth, like other planets, revolved around the sun. For the next 400 hundred years, wise men contented themselves with the belief that our solar system was at least the center of the Milky Way galaxy. However, in 1918, Harlow Shapoely showed that our solar system was actually off to the edge. Nevertheless, the wise men said, our galaxy must surely be at the center of the universe. But in 1929, Edwin Hubble demonstrated it was not. Hubble discovered that the universe was and is expanding. The observation that every galaxy is moving away from every other galaxy and spreading out yielded the big bang theory. Recently, the big bang theory has been challenged by Alan Guth's theory of the inflationary universe. Now, Andrai Linde, among others, has put forth the idea of multiple universes. The idea of multiple universes is staggering, even for scientists. This new knowledge is modifying the world of physics and changing the way we look at things.

The observations of actions, reactions, and relationships, have established natural laws, theories, and principles in all fields of science. Hypotheses are stated, data are gathered and analyzed, conclusions are drawn, and the data support or reject the hypotheses. When replicated, these observations add to the degree of probability that something is a fact. For example, in educational research, data are not accepted unless they reach the .05 level of significance, or 95 times out of a hundred, the same data will yield the same results. Historical facts are supported or not supported based on the evidence

Table 2C
Descriptive Knowledge (Truth) Continuum (Validated by Observations)

Is the truth (what was, is, will be) established?

FICTION <--> FACT

No or inconsistent	High and consistent
number of observations.	number of observations.
0% probability.	100% probability.

---

of the data.

Descriptive knowledge can range on a continuum with no or inconsistent observations and low probability at one end, to consistent observations and high probability on the other end. See Table 2C: Descriptive Knowledge (Truth) Continuum.

Technological Knowledge (Truth) Continuum

Technological knowledge establishes the efficiency and effectiveness of performances, processes, methods, techniques, and practices, and their accompanying knowledge, skills and abilities and values to bring about what is desired. Technological knowledge includes knowledge of practice, and practice itself. One must know what to do and how to do it before performing a task. One must try out or perform a task to gain knowledge of what it is like to do it, to feel it, to experience it, and to observe and validate the efficiency and effectiveness of the process and its results. It is in the practice of medicine that physicians learn from experience as to how to adapt their knowledge of medicine to the individual health peculiarities of patients. It is in the practice of teaching that teachers learn how to tailor the subject and their methods to their particular students. Teachers learn how to adjust their style of delivery, the activities they require their students to do, the materials selected for study, etc., to accommodate, for example, the range of learners in the class (gifted, disadvantaged, physically disabled, etc.). Thus, from experience, there arises a body of knowledge as to *how to do* to make teaching and learning more efficient and effective.

Technological knowledge can be viewed on a continuum of minimum efficiency and effectiveness on one end to maximum efficiency and effectiveness on the other end. See Table 2D: Technological Knowledge

Table 2D
Technological Knowledge (Truth) Continuum (Validated by Observations)

Is the truth (efficiency, effectiveness) established?

MINIMUM <---> MAXIMUM

Knowledge of practice.	Knowledge of practice.
Efficiency and effectiveness	Efficiency and effectiveness
in practice.	in practice.

(Truth) Continuum.

Implications for Curriculum

According to Mason (1996, p. 264), many believe the traditional curriculum fails to meet the needs of students in a complex, technologically advanced, interdependent world. Constructivists contend that schools are *out of sync* with the society they are designed to serve. Proponents of integrated models of curriculum view integrated curriculum as a means to resolve this problem and revive the moribund contemporary school.

The conceptual framework (instructional system) facilitates the integration of subject matter. The inputs of symbolic, prescriptive, descriptive, and technological information/content provide the opportunity for teachers to introduce subject matter drawn from other disciplines. Information/content should be introduced as co-requisite subject matter for learning the discipline and for holistic learning. Educators have begun to realize that students are better educated when they know how knowledge and skills are combined and used in the real world. It is not enough to teach mathematics, science, English, etc., for their own sake, but to show its applications in related areas and to the broader society. To do so, makes the curriculum more relevant and worthwhile.

Recent trends to integrate subject matter such as, mathematics, science, and technology and vocational and academic areas are indications of the need to integrate subject matter. If the teacher does not present the connection between knowledge fields, the student is left to make their own connections to the real world, assuming of course that the student will at sometime, make these connections. This is not likely in the traditional curriculum. The time to teach the integrated information/content is when the subject matter is being studied.

Symbolic, prescriptive, descriptive, and technological inputs provide for this integration and are essential for holistic learning. These inputs can be related to the four domains of objectives: cognitive, affective, psychomotor and behavioral domains. Descriptive information/content (what was, is, will be), is an input to the cognitive domain objectives. Prescriptive information/content (what ought to be) is an input to the affective domain objectives. Technological information/content (know what and how to do) is an input to the psychomotor domain objectives. Symbolic information/content (signs, symbols, language used to communicate all information) is an input to the behavioral domain objectives. See Fig. 2.3 Relationship of Information Inputs to Domain Objectives.

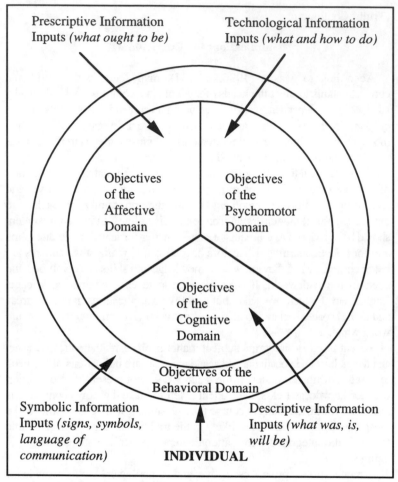

Fig. 2.3 Relationship of Information Inputs to Domain Objectives

Fig. 2.3 shows the general relationship of information inputs to the domain objectives. Descriptive information (what was, is, will be) is an input to the cognitive domain objectives. Prescriptive information (what ought to be) is an input to the affective domain objectives. Technological information (what and how to do) is an input to the psychomotor domain objectives and symbolic information (signs, symbols, language used to communicate all knowledge) is an input to the overall behavioral domain.

Summary

The conceptual framework (instructional system) inputs are delineated as symbolic, prescriptive, descriptive, and technological information/content (others' knowledge). Symbolic information/content is seen as an input of *signs, symbols, and language* used to communicate all information. Prescriptive information/content is seen as an input of *what ought to be*. Descriptive information/content is seen as an input of *what was, is, and will be*. Technological information/content is seen as an input of knowing *what to do and how to do it* as well as knowledge gained from experiences.

Knowledge (other's knowledge as information/content) is seen as being derived from truths. These are analytic truths (validated by consensus) and experiential truths (validated by observation). Symbolic and prescriptive knowledge are derived from analytic truths and descriptive and technological knowledge are derived from experiential truths.

The conceptual framework facilitates the integration of subject matter. Recent trends to integrate content from various disciplines support the constructivist view that students learn best when ideas are connected to one another.

Each input of information/content is classified as relating to a domain of the individual: prescriptive information to the affective domain; descriptive information to the cognitive domain; technological information to the psychomotor domain; and symbolic information to all domains as well as the overall behavioral domain. All four information inputs are seen as essential in a curriculum for holistic learning.

Questions to Consider

1. What implications does the conceptual framework have for current practice in utilizing cognitive, affective, and psychomotor objectives?
2. Why should *knowledge* not be a subcategory in the taxonomy of objectives in the cognitive domain?
3. Is there a difference between information and knowledge?
4. Why is information considered to be others' knowledge?
5. What are the commonalities and differences between symbolic and prescriptive information/content inputs?
6. What are the commonalities and differences between descriptive and technological information/content inputs?
7. How would you define truth?
8. What implications does the conceptual framework have for curriculum?

9. How do the four information/content inputs facilitate the ideas of constructivism?
10. What questions do you have?

References

1. Bloom, Benjamin. S. (Ed.), Englehart, Max. D., Furst, Edward. J., Hill, Walker H. and Krathwohl, David R., 1956. *Taxonomy of educational objectives. The classification of educational goals, Handbook I: Cognitive domain.* New York: Longmans, Green, Co.
2. Dugger, William E. Jr. (Director), January, 1997. *Technology for all Americans.* A project of the International Technology Education Association to develop standards for K-12 technology education. Blacksburg, Virginia.
3. Hauenstein, A. Dean, 1972. *Curriculum planning for behavioral development.* Worthington, Ohio: Charles A. Jones Publishing Company.
4. Maccia, Elizabeth Steiner, 1965. *Curriculum theory and policy.* Presented to the American Educational Research Association Meeting, Chicago, 1965 (Columbus, Ohio: Bureau of Educational Research and Service, Occasional Paper No. 65-176). The Ohio State University. (Mimeographed).
5. Mason, Terrence C. 1996. *Integrated curricula: Potential and problems.* Journal of Teacher Education, September-October, Vol. 47, No. 4. American Association of Colleges for Teacher Education and Corwin Press, Inc.
6. Towers, Edward R., Lux, Donald G., and Ray, Willis E., 1966. *A rationale and structure for industrial arts subject matter.* A Joint Project of The Ohio State University and the University of Illinois. Sponsored by U. S. Office of Education, Bureau of Research, Division of Adult and Vocational Research. Columbus, Ohio.

Chapter 3

The Cognitive Domain: Redefined

Introduction

Seldom has there been a publication so widely accepted as a part of the teachers' education as Bloom's et al. *Taxonomy of Educational Objectives. The Classification of Educational Goals, Handbook I: Cognitive Domain.* It would be unusual to find a teacher education institution or school system that did not in some form use the taxonomy of cognitive objectives. Nevertheless, this educational icon falls short in several areas of applicability when evaluated on three aspects: 1) terminology, 2) hierarchy, and 3) delineation of intellectual abilities and skills. Hence, it has been necessary to establish reasonable taxonomic rules as external criteria against which Bloom's et al. taxonomy can be critically analyzed and evaluated.

These rules deal with the criteria of applicability, total inclusiveness, and mutual exclusiveness of categories and subcategories, order and hierarchy of categories, and communication of the intent of the objectives. Discrepancies between these taxonomic criteria and Bloom's et al. taxonomy are identified and discussed, and revisions are made. Composite modifications are embodied in a redefined taxonomy of cognitive objectives.

The redefined taxonomy is a step in improving the taxonomy to serve the teaching profession. It is assumed the reader has some knowledge of the *Taxonomy of Educational Objectives. The Classification of Educational Goals, Handbook I: Cognitive Domain.* If not, the reader should become acquainted with a condensed version of the taxonomy in Appendix A.

The next chapters present redefined taxonomies for the affective and psychomotor domains and a composite taxonomy for the behavioral domain. Overall, an attempt is made to develop taxonomies that reflect thinking abilities and skills and the learning process, both in terminology and process. The intent of the redefined taxonomies is to help teachers enable students to develop their intellect, to develop their critical, reflective, and problem solving thinking abilities and skills--to help students think for themselves.

Before proceeding with the discussion of the taxonomy for the cognitive domain, it will be useful to consider some definitions, terminology, and common criteria for structuring a taxonomy.

Definitions

Taxonomy--a classification system that establishes the hierarchy of the parts to other parts and the parts to the whole. It is an orderly classification of items according to their presumed natural relationships. For example, in classifying insects, they would be classified according to their characteristics. One would not include arachnids.

Ability--natural, innate capability, aptitude.

Skill--ability to use one's knowledge effectively and readily in execution or performance, an acquired proficiency.

Terminology

Since we cannot observe intellectual thought processes of a student, it is important for teachers to have behavioral evidence from which thinking abilities and skills can be inferred. The most common observations that provide this evidence are what students say and do and products produced by students. Since we use the taxonomy to classify observed intellectual abilities and skills, the terms used in the categories and subcategories must be able to be expressed in behavioral action terms. For example, teachers need to be able to identify an intellectual ability or skill when it is happening, e.g., interpreting, clarifying, hypothesizing, etc. It is in the behaviors of thinking or products of thinking that objectives are realized. A test for identifying an intellectual ability or skill is to add *ing* to the terms, thus, comprehension--comprehending, translation--translating, analysis--analyzing, evaluation--evaluating, etc. The terms should be able to be expressed also as verbs for learning outcomes, e.g., comprehension--comprehends, translation--translates, etc.

The terminology used to classify intellectual abilities and skills should be generic, that is, be applicable to any situation or context. By focusing on generic intellectual abilities and skills, the taxonomy will maintain stability that relates to any context. For example, in using *analysis,* one would not list in a taxonomy, the kinds or types of items one analyzes, e.g., analyzes elements, analyzes relationships, analyzes organizational principles. The overall generic objective and behavioral ability is still *analysis.* What one needs to know to analyze elements (in a specific context) may be different from what one needs to know to analyze organizational principles (a different context). The objective and behavioral ability is still *analysis*. The context will vary with the content being taught at the time.

Taxonomic Criteria/Conditions

As indicated, a taxonomy is a classification system that establishes the hierarchy of the parts, to other parts and the parts to the whole. The taxonomy is described as a hierarchy because lower order categories are prerequisites to higher order categories. For example, conceptualization of a concept is a prerequisite to comprehension of the idea in a broader context and comprehension, in turn, is a prerequisite to the application of the idea. In constructing or evaluating a taxonomy, it is necessary to have some common taxonomic criteria and conditions against which it can be judged. These requisites are listed here as *rules*.

Rule 1. The taxonomy must have *applicability*, e.g., be relevant to the function for which it will be used. When the taxonomy is used to classify overt behaviors (abilities and skills) and products of behavior reflecting knowledge, the terms must *be able to be expressed* as verbs or gerund nouns (words ending in *ing*). A test for this is to add *ing* to the terms, thus, translation--translating, interpretation--interpreting, etc. Content concepts, principles, or phenomena should not be listed as a category or sub-category.

Rule 2. The taxonomy, as a whole, must be *totally inclusive*--the components represent all categories in a given context, e.g., intellectual abilities and skills. The categories must be comprehensive. There should be no error of omission among the parts or between the parts and the whole. As a test, there should nothing you can think of (any behavior exhibiting an intellectual ability or skill) that would not be able to be classified under one of the categories or subcategories.

Rule 3. Categories of the taxonomy must be *mutually exclusive*--there is no overlap between categories or within subcategories of a category. Each category stands independent from the other categories in intent and function. As a test, the subcategories are explicit enough to give definition to the category and the terms used are not repeated within a category. A sub-term in one category can be used in another category, but not within the same category. As a principle, it is better not to repeat a term in any category to avoid confusion.

Rule 4. The categories must be arranged following a consistent *principle of order*, e.g., from simple to complex, easy to difficult, concrete to abstract, prerequisite to requisite, cause-effect, etc. If a category is

Table 3A
Abbreviated Taxonomy of Cognitive Objectives

Redefined Cognitive Taxonomy	Cognitive Taxonomy (Bloom et al. 1956)
Intellectual Abilities and Skills	*Knowledge*
1.0 Conceptualization	**1.00 Knowledge**
1.1 Identification	1.10 Knowledge of specifics
1.2 Definition	1.20 Knowledge of ways and means of dealing with specifics
1.3 Generalization	1.30 Knowledge of universals and abstractions in a field
	Intellectual Abilities and Skills
2.0 Comprehension	**2.00 Comprehension**
2.1 Translation	2.10 Translation
2.2 Interpretation	2.20 Interpretation
2.3 Extrapolation	2.30 Extrapolation
3.0 Application	**3.00 Application**
3.1 Clarification	
3.2 Solution	
	4.00 Analysis
4.0 Evaluation	4.10 Analysis of elements
4.1 Analysis	4.20 Analysis of relationships
4.2 Qualification	4.30 Analysis of organizational principles
5.0 Synthesis	**5.00 Synthesis**
5.1 Hypothesis	5.10 Production of a unique communication
5.2 Resolution	5.20 Production of a plan, or proposed set of operations
	5.30 Derivation of a set of abstract relations
	6.00 Evaluation
	6.10 Judgements in terms of internal evidence
	6.20 Judgements in terms of external evidence

subdivided, it must have at least two subcategories which follow the same principle of order.

Rule 5. The *terms* used to identify categories and subcategories should *communicate* the idea and be representative of those used in the field. A test for this is, *Do the generic terms communicate the intent of the objectives to teachers in the field?*

Coding and Process

The major categories, called first order objectives, can be designated as 1.0, 2.0, 3.0, etc. A subcategory is called a second order objective, e.g., 2.0-- 2.1, 2.2, 2.3, etc. A further breakdown within an order would be sub-coded within the taxonomy, e.g., 2.1--2.1.1, 2.1.2, 2.1..3, etc., 2.2--2.2.1, 2.2.2, 2.2.3 etc. In developing the second order of objectives, the same Rules 1-5 apply. For example, 2.0 Comprehension (is now the whole) and any sub-orders established must have applicability, be totally inclusive of comprehension, be mutually exclusive of each other, be arranged following a consistent principle of order, and communicate the intent. The same procedure and criteria are used for any third order classification of behavior. The coding, criteria and process would continue ad infinitum.

Redefined Taxonomy of Cognitive Objectives

Modifications of the taxonomy are posited for consideration. The redefined taxonomy of abbreviated cognitive objectives is shown in Table 3A: Abbreviated Taxonomy of Cognitive Objectives and is aligned with Bloom's et al. abbreviated taxonomy of cognitive objectives, for ease of comparison. Rationales for the redefined categories and objectives follow.

Taxonomic Terminology Error

It is a taxonomic error to mix unlike species, such as apples and oranges. In reviewing Bloom's cognitive domain objectives there appears to be a mix of species, or more accurately, a mix of unlike terminologies denoting species. The 1.00 category of *Knowledge* is mixed with categories 2.00 through 6.00 *Intellectual Abilities and Skills*, namely: comprehension, application, analysis, synthesis, and evaluation. See Table 3A.

According to Rule 1: Applicability, knowledge might be expressed in a behavioral form as *knowing*. If that is the case, then it is in conflict with Rule 3: Mutually Exclusive. All of the second order categories of *Knowledge* are

Table 3B
Summary of Taxonomic Rule Violations

Taxonomic Rules	Bloom et al. Taxonomy: Cognitive Objectives	Rule Violations
Rule 1 **Applicability** Relevant to function. Gerund noun.	**Knowledge** **1.00 Knowledge** 1.10 Knowledge of specifics 1.20 Knowledge of ways and means of dealing with specifics	**1.00 Knowledge** #1. Knowledge is not a gerund noun. Knowledge is mixed with abilities and skills.
Rule 2 **Total inclusiveness** Represents all categories in a given context.	1.30 Knowledge of universals and abstractions in a field **Intellectual Abilities and Skills** **2.00 Comprehension**	#2 Knowledge is not relevant to function. #3. Subcategories are not mutually exclusive, all are *knowledge of's*. **2.00 Comprehension** (Acceptable as is).
Rule 3 **Mutual exclusiveness** No overlap between categories or within subcategories.	2.10 Translation 2.20 Interpretation 2.30 Extrapolation **3.00 Application** **4.00 Analysis** 4.10 Analysis of elements	**3.00 Application** #2 and #4. Lacks specificty of subcategories. **4.00 Analysis** #1 and #3. All subcategories are not applicable nor
Rule 4 **Principle of order** e.g., Simple to complex. Prerequisite to requisite. Must have at least 2 subcategories.	4.20 Analysis of relationships 4.30 Analysis of organizational principles **5.00 Synthesis** 5.10 Production of a unique communication 5.20 Production of a plan, or a proposed set of operations 5.30 Derivation of a set of abstract relations	mutually exclusive, all are *analysis of's*. **5.00 Synthesis** #3. All subcategories not mutually exclusive. #4. Synthesis is not a prerequisite to evaluation.
Rule 5 **Communicate intent** Identifiable behavior in the classroom.	**6.00 Evaluation** 6.10 Judgements in terms of internal evidence 6.20 Judgements in terms of external evidence	**6.00 Evaluation** #1 and #3. All subcategories are not applicable nor mutually exclusive, both are *judgements in....*

stated as *Knowledge of's* . . ., e.g., knowledge of specifics, knowledge of ways and means of dealing with specifics, and knowledge of universals and abstractions in a field. One cannot use *knowledge* (or knowing) to define itself. The second order objectives are not mutually exclusive.

The focus of Bloom et al. *knowledge* objectives is on the types or forms of knowledge to be acquired rather than on behaviors (intellectual abilities and skills) which enable and verify the acquisition of knowledge. The *possession* of knowledge *is not* an ability or skill. The *acquiring* of knowledge *is* an intellectual ability and skill. To be taxonomically consistent all categories and subcategories should be expressed in relation to abilities and skills (Rule 2: Totally Inclusive and Rule 3: Mutually Exclusive). A condensed version of the rule violations of each of the Bloom et al. cognitive objectives is shown in Table 3B: Summary of Taxonomic Rule Violations.

Information, Content, and Knowledge Defined

Even though Bloom et al. indicate that what is meant by knowledge is the remembering and recalling of information, the use of the term *knowledge* confuses the objective. To alleviate this terminology problem, it may be useful to provide some clarification of the terms: information, content, and knowledge. It is important to discern the difference between content and knowledge. *Information* is defined herein as the *totality of humankind's recorded knowledge,*--that which is found in libraries, media centers, museums, the Internet, paper files, and the human mind, external to our own. *Content* is defined here as *selected information* in reference to a particular subject, content or topic, such as subject matter selected from books, articles, films, tapes, computer files, paper files, and other humans. Content or subject matter is usually selected to inform one about a specific subject or topic. *Information and content are external* to the individual whereas *knowledge is internal* or intrinsic. Content presented in a book or on the Internet does not become knowledge to us until we have read or viewed it, garnered some important points, attached some meaning to them, and gained some general understanding of the content.

Acquiring knowledge is an assimilation process. To get knowledge we intellectually process information into meanings and understandings. We integrate the new content with what we already know. For example, the content (ideas, concepts, and principles) we retain from reading a book or the Internet becomes knowledge to us and awaits recall or use.

Sometimes knowledge is not retained in a form that is readily available for recall and may be forgotten. On the other hand, some would argue that we do not forget anything, things are only misfiled in our memory. If we can not recall it, it is no longer useable knowledge to us. An appropriate verbal or tacit cue, however, may stimulate recall.

Information/Content (Others' Knowledge) as Input

In Bloom et al. *Taxonomy of Educational Objectives: Cognitive Domain* the category of *Knowledge* is an excellent classification of the types and forms in which information (others' knowledge) may be presented or encountered. These information categories are: terminology, specific facts, conventions, trends and sequences, classifications and categories, criteria, methodology, principles and generalizations, and theories and structure. Primarily, these deal with what kinds of information students should have access to as opposed to the abilities to acquire and use knowledge. In the redefined taxonomy, information/content is seen as the essential *input* to the cognitive process objectives. Given information/content as an input, the process objectives to develop intellectual abilities and skills in the redefined taxonomy are conceptualization, comprehension, application, evaluation, and synthesis, which in turn, yields an outcome, a knowledgeable individual. See Fig. 3.1: Instructional System for the Cognitive Domain.

If one agrees that information and content (others' knowledge) are external and are input stimuli to acquiring knowledge, then knowledge cannot be included in a category of intellectual abilities and skills. *Knowledge* cannot be external and internal at the same time. The contention that knowledge is not part of the cognitive domain taxonomy is further supported by the fact that when objectives are utilized by practitioners, they take the form of *conditions* or *givens* (Mager 1984, 50). In writing objectives, *knowledge* is an essential input before using it. For example, *After viewing a film about color (input), be able to* identify primary colors, analogous colors, etc., or Given a list of colors (input), the student will . . . The point is that content is external; it is input to the learner and does not become knowledge until the learner has had some cognitive experience with it. Thus, *knowledge* can *not* be a category in a taxonomy of objectives representing cognitive abilities and skills. Information and content, however, are the key inputs to the cognitive processes.

In reference to cognitive objectives, Bloom, et al. indicate they are not attempting to classify the particular subject matter or content, but are classifying the intended behavior of students--the ways in which individuals are to act (Bloom et al. 1956, 12). However, the use of phrases *knowledge of specifics, knowledge of ways and means of dealing with specifics, etc.,*

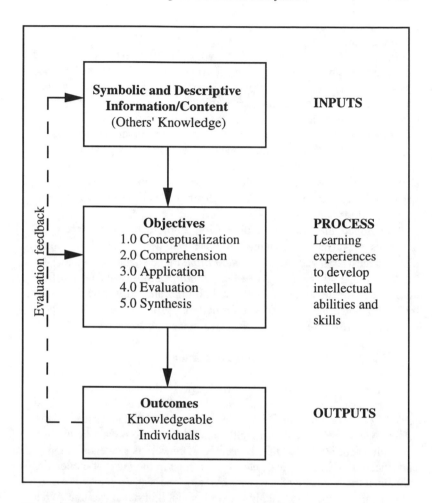

Fig. 3.1 Instructional System for the Cognitive Domain

Fig. 3.1 shows an instructional system for cognitive with symbolic and descriptive information/content (others' knowledge) as inputs to the process objectives for developing intellectual abilities and skills of conceptualization, comprehension, application, evaluation, and synthesis that produce knowledgeable individuals as an output. Evaluation feedback provides for adjustment of the information/content inputs and process objectives.

do imply particular subject matter or content and is vague in expressing how individuals are to act.

Bloom et al. (1956, 29) explain that, by knowledge, what is meant is that the student can give evidence that he/she remembers, either by recognizing or by recalling, some idea or phenomenon with which he/she has had experience in the educational process. Further, for their taxonomy purposes, they define knowledge as little more than the remembering of the idea or phenomenon in a form limited to the ability to remember and recall something. To be taxonomically consistent with intellectual abilities and skills, the knowledge objective should be *remembering* and *recalling* or some other term denoting an ability and skill as opposed to: terminology, specific facts, conventions, trends, and so forth, which represent content and are not abilities or skills.

It is hoped that the above discussion is more than an exercise in semantics. An attempt has been made to clarify *knowledge* and place it in its proper context as an *information/content input* to the cognitive domain. To fill the void, it is suggested that *conceptualization* should be the first objective in the hierarchy of intellectual abilities and skills. The following brief discussion of how concepts are formed may provide additional support for *conceptualization* as the 1.0 objective in the revised taxonomy.

Concept Formation

A concept is a mental construct of an idea derived from specific instances or occurances in the effort to understand what it represents. Caine and Caine (1997, 173) state that a concept is an underlying idea that gives meaning to a fact. A concept cannot be literally handed from one person to another, although teachers try to do this frequently. A concept is a categorization or classification of events, ideas, etc. It is formed in the mind of the learner rather than transmitted by the teacher. All a teacher can do is to express his or her own concept of something is to talk about it or demonstrate it. What is transmitted are words or actions. Those words and actions may not give the learner a clear picture at all. The easiest way for a teacher to make the concept known is to present an exemplar of the concept. The easiest way for learners to formulate the concept is to perceive it for themselves in all of its variations. Each person has to construct his/her own concepts from experience with an array of examples and non-examples. It is an error to believe that communication is the transmission of meaning between people. Meanings themselves cannot be transmitted, but meaningful sets of symbols can. We can consider signs and symbols as information. We can also assume that signs and symbols are only meaningful when there is consensus as to what they symbolize and when the pattern of their presentation is consistent with established conventions.

Woodruff (1961, 63) indicates that when, through experience, we get a mental picture in our mind of one of the objects or forces which make up our world, we have a concept, which immediately becomes our *set* for any further perception of the same thing. He explains that the human mind is a depository for all our experiences, and as such, the record is a composite of meanings or understandings, feelings and the values and preferences it produces, and the symbols or languages related to them. This combination of meanings, values and symbols is a concept. A concept is a meaning which is at least partially organized into a recognizable idea.

Woodruff explains that learning begins with the senses. It begins with some form of personal contact with an object, event or circumstance in life. The contacts occur through our sense organs: eyes, ears, nose, mouth, and skin. Through personal association and interaction with any thing in the world, the individual gets a mental impression of what it represents. This is called a percept or perception. As experience accumulates with the referent, the picture includes what it looks like, sounds like, smells like, tastes like, feels like, etc. and what it does or produces. These interactions and observations make up the formation of a concept. Each new mental picture of some thing is checked against the pictures already in the mind, and worked into them. From these constantly occurring acts of perception, we formulate our concepts which give us understandings of life. Understanding, by definition, is the forming of a generalization from particulars.

Woodruff (1961, 78) indicates that as a concept forms in our minds, we learn symbols for the whole concept as well as for each of its parts or qualities, and these symbols also become part of the concept. Language is made up of symbols which stand for thoughts. We use vocal symbols every time we speak. This is the most direct way of communicating our thoughts. There are written symbols to stand for the vocal ones, so we can put our thoughts in writing and let others read them. Sometimes, we use signs and symbols to stand for our thoughts, such as: +, $, ?, 3, and colors and shapes that stand for various ideas, e.g., red--danger/warning, octagon--stop sign.

Signs and symbols have no significance in themselves. They simply stand for something in the mind of a person. The concept always comes first. After one has developed a concept, a sign or symbol *handle* is needed for it so the idea can be referenced. A sign or symbol has no meaning unless it is connected with an idea. Signs and symbols are learned by memorizing them, usually through repetition and drill. Since we can learn to speak, hear, write, and read, we make up names for what we perceive in the world. We use these names to communicate to others what we are *seeing* in our minds (our concepts). We do this orally, in writing, or by using gestures. We try to agree on what sign or name we will use for each idea, so we can understand each other. Meaningful sets of symbols transmit meanings, such as: home, school, mother, zygote, December, Miami, and so forth, as well as feelings and one's preferences about them.

Objective 1.0 Conceptualization

When new information/content is presented, the initial experience of the presentation should enable one to remember and recall the referent (bit of information to be acquired, idea to be learned), that is, form a concept of the referent and its particulars in a specific context. Without the initial conceptualization experience, one would not be able to remember or recall the idea. Thus, the first experience with a referent must enable the individual to conceive, that is, to associate the concept with its signs, symbols and meaning--to conceptualize the referent in a given context.

According to Shepard (1989, 5-6), current models of learning based on cognitive psychology contend that learners gain understanding when they construct their own knowledge and develop their own cognitive maps of the interconnectedness among facts and concepts. Real learning cannot be spoon-fed one skill at a time.

The intellectual abilities to be developed to enable conceptualization are *identification* of the referent, *definition* of the particulars of the referent and *generalization*, which yield the initial understanding of the concept. Being able to identify, define and generalize the particulars of an idea, object or phenomenon in a specific context facilitates conceptualization and thus, facilitates memory and recall.

The remembering and recall test descriptors commonly associated with the *knowledge* category are terms such as: define, name, list, identify, and describe (Gronlund 1970, 21). Thus, in utilizing the knowledge objective, these experiences and tests are already apparent in the professional literature on objectives. For clarity and better communication, it is posited that the first encounter with new information be termed *conceptualization* with subcategories of identification, definition, and generalization.

For greater clarity, the conceptualization categories are defined as follows: (1) identification--ability to associate, remember and recall specific signs and symbols in relation to ideas, objects, and phenomena in a given context, (2) definition--ability to discern (fix the identity of) the essential qualities, limits, and meaning of a concept, and (3) generalization--ability to integrate the particulars of an idea, object, or phenomena in order to be able to communicate the overall composition and nature of the concept.

It seems reasonable to suggest that conceptualization is a prerequisite to comprehension. According to Marzano et al. (1988, 33), concept formation is the foundation for other processes. For example, when students encounter new content, they must establish the essential concepts before they can comprehend more densely organized information. Thus, comprehension relies on the ability to conceptualize--to identify, define, and generalize content into a meaningful idea and understanding in a specific context.

The term *conceptualization* is precise and descriptive as a 1.0 category in the cognitive domain objectives, i.e., conceptualization, comprehension, application, evaluation, and synthesis. The redefined taxonomy of the first category of cognitive objectives is posited in Table 3C: Conceptualization. The redefined taxonomy is shown in Table 3I: Redefined Taxonomy of Educational Objectives: Cognitive Domain.

Table 3C
Conceptualization (Defined)

1.0 Conceptualization. Ability to identify, define, and generalize an idea in a specific context.

    1.1 **Identification.** Ability to associate, remember and recall specific signs and symbols in relation to ideas, objects, or phenomena in a given context (e.g., name the sunshine state, identify the arm bones, state the primary colors, list the steps in a process, label an item, identify an acronym, recognize a body gesture).
    Applicable test descriptors: identifies, names, states, labels, lists, relates, recognizes.

    1.2 **Definition**. Ability to discern the essential qualities, limits, and meaning of a concept (e.g., define a term--outline, state the characteristics of some phenomena--electricity).
    Applicable test descriptors: defines, relates, states, matches.

    1.3 **Generalization**. Ability to integrate the particulars of an idea, object, or phenomena in order to be able to communicate the overall composition and nature of the concept (e.g., describe an object--mirror, explain a term--switch, outline a process).
    Applicable test descriptors: describes, reproduces, outlines, writes, explains, generalizes.

Conceptualization and Comprehension

In this redefined taxonomy, the Bloom et al. category of 2.00 *Comprehension* (including translation, interpretation, and extrapolation) is acceptable because it meets all of the taxonomic criteria. It is reviewed here for its continuity in the redefined taxonomy. A brief review of *comprehension* indicates that conceptualization and comprehension are compatible and not in conflict in the redefined taxonomy. According to Bloom et al. (1956, 89) the first type of comprehension behavior is *translation*, which means that an individual can put a communication into other language, into other terms, or into another form of communication. It usually involves the giving of meaning to the various parts of a communication, taken in isolation, although such meanings may be determined by the context in which the ideas appear.

Bloom et al. (1956, 90) state that the second type of comprehension behavior is *interpretation* which involves dealing with a communication as a configuration of ideas, the comprehension of which may require reordering of the ideas into a new configuration in the mind of the individual. This also includes thinking about the relative importance of the ideas, their interrelationships, and their relevance to generalizations implied or described in the original communication. The third comprehension ability is *extrapolation* which includes the making of estimates or predictions based on understandings of the trends, tendencies, or conditions described in the communication. It may also involve the making of inferences with respect to implications, consequences, corollaries, and effects, which are in accordance with the conditions described in the communication.

The distinction between conceptualization and comprehension is that conceptualization relates to the transforming of new information/content into ideas and understandings (concepts), whereas comprehension implies the assimilation of the newly acquired concept(s) from a specific context to a similar or different context. The integration of a new concept with prior knowledge facilitates translation and interpretation in the comprehension category and also facilitates the concept building process.

Implications

If one accepts the premise that teachers are *facilitators* as opposed to *fountains of knowledge,* it is incumbent upon teachers to ensure that, when new information/content is presented, the learning experiences promote the development of concepts and conceptualization abilities. Some teachers use techniques such as, mnemonics to help students increase their ability to associate, remember and recall concepts, objects, phenomena and other knowledge. Teachers also explain, use analogies, examples, and demonstrations to help students perceive similarities and differences, determine what something is or is not, and perceive the nature of things in a given context. The use of such techniques encourage students to construct their own mental images, connections and meanings--to develop a concept. The intent of this redefinition is to focus Objective 1.0 on the acquisition of concepts by the students, i.e., the students can identify, define, and generalize particulars of the content concepts in a specific context, rather than the presentation of content about specifics, ways and means, etc., by the teacher.

When teachers focus on the delivery or coverage of subject matter as opposed to the development of concepts, students are shortchanged. Teachers sometimes erroneously expect students to *comprehend* something without providing them experiences critical to the development of the prerequisite concepts necessary to comprehension. Students may not recognize the vocabulary, signs, or definitions the teacher is using. Thus, the student can not conceptualize clearly and tunes-out. Similarly, at the application level, a teacher may demonstrate how to solve a math problem and then expect students to *apply* that information (the teachers' knowledge) before the students have conceptualized and comprehend the problem or procedures leading to the solution. To skip over essential prerequisites is to ensure frustration and possible failure on the part of the student.

A contributing factor to the current decline of SAT scores, poor reading and math skills, and academic achievement, may be the preoccupation with the teaching of subject matter per se. Teacher education institutions may have contributed to this problem by what they teach about cognitive *knowledge* objectives, i.e., emphasizing content instead of the acquisition of concepts.

The above discussion may cause some teachers to take a second look at what and how they are teaching, and what intellectual abilities and skills their students are developing. It may also stimulate other educators to examine cognitive learning theory, learning styles and research.

2.0 Comprehension Objectives

The category 2.00 *Comprehension* (Bloom et al.) is accepted as meeting the new taxonomic criteria. This category is presented below for review and continuity. An overall definition of comprehension has been added along with second order definitions and examples. See Table 3D: Comprehension.

Table 3D
Comprehension (Redefined)

2.0 Comprehension. Ability to translate and interpret ideas, and extrapolate content information.

    2.1 **Translation**. Ability to put communication into another form (e.g., state problems in own words, read a musical score, translate words and phrases from a foreign language, describe a diagram/drawing, relate the meaning of a cartoon).
    Applicable test descriptors: converts, translates, draws, diagrams, relates, describes.

    2.2 **Interpretation**. Ability to explain ideas and interrelationships (e.g., tell your own interpretation of an idea or set of facts, write a report explaining a set of data, explain a blueprint, represent by means of art).
    Applicable test descriptors: gives examples, paraphrases, explains, interprets, tells, represents.

    2.3 **Extrapolation**. Ability to make inferences from information (e.g., make a forecast from a given set of data, project what is needed to meet an objective, identify a trend, derive a principle).
    Applicable test descriptors: infers, projects, predicts, forecasts, estimates, extrapolates, derives, deduces.

3.0 Application Objectives

Category 3.00 *Application* is accepted as meeting the taxonomic criteria as a first order category. To help facilitate the development of intellectual abilities and skills and the learning process, second order objectives have been added to 3.0 Application. The 3.00 *Application* category (Bloom et al.) does not specify any component intellectual abilities and skills.

As per Bloom et al. application is defined as the ability to apply principles to actual situations. Greater clarity of application abilities and skills can be provided by expanding the category to include second order objectives. The addition of 3.1 Clarification and 3.2 Solution indicate that applying has as least two generic abilities and skills or sub-objectives.

Application typically deals with singular problems and situations. A problem is a question that needs a answer. When a teacher asks *What is the problem here*? or the student says *I don't understand the problem*, this is an indication that clarification is needed. There is a need to intellectually identify and isolate the elements of the problem or situation from its surrounding context to define the problem or situation. See Table 3E: Application. See also, Table 3B: Summary of Taxonomic Rule Violations.

Solution means that appropriate principles and procedures have been identified and used to solve or deal with a specific problem or situation.

Table 3E
Application (Redefined)

3.0 Application. Ability to clarify a problem or situation and use appropriate principles and procedures to solve a specific problem or situation.

    3.1 **Clarification.** Ability to isolate the elements of a singular problem or situation from its surrounding context (e.g., discern relevant and nonrelevant elements, identify the specifics of the problem, define a problem).

    Applicable test descriptors: identifies, discerns, defines, clarifies, isolates, diagnoses.

    3.2 **Solution**. Ability to use appropriate principles and procedures in the solution of a specific problem or situation. (e.g., use math and accounting principles to balance a checkbook, use Ohm's law to compute voltage or amperage or resistance, use grammar rules to write sentences and paragraphs, use orthographic principles and procedures to construct a drawing, use the scientific process to do an experiment).

    Applicable test descriptors: determines, decides, resolves, answers, solves, shows, produces, uses, experiments.

Hierarchy of Bloom's et al. Objectives 4.00-6.00: Redefined

The objectives 1.0 Conceptualization, 2.0 Comprehension, and 3.0 Application are classified herein as *short term* objectives. These can probably be achieved by a student within a lesson. The redefined objectives 4.0 Evaluation (includes analysis and qualification) and 5.0 Synthesis (includes hypothesis and resolution) are seen as *long term* objectives. These are presented in turn.

Bloom's et al. taxonomy is questioned with regard to the specificity and sequence and/or hierarchy, namely the specificity and placement of 4.00 *Analysis,* 5.00 *Synthesis*, and 6.00 *Evaluation*. Categories 4.00 Analysis,

5.00 Synthesis, and 6.00 Evaluation do not meet the criteria of Rule 2: Totally Inclusive, and Rule 3: Mutually Exclusive, and Rule 4: Principle of Order, and Rule 5: Communication of the intent of the objectives. The redefined hierarchy and specificity provide better communication and better serve the critical thinking, reflective thinking, problem solving, and decision making processes as well as teaching and learning. See Table 3B: Summary of Taxonomic Rule Violations.

4.0 Evaluation

As per Bloom et al., evaluation is a judgement based on internal evidence of external criteria. Bloom et al. place 6.00 *Evaluation* as the highest level category.

The category 5.00 *Synthesis* is not a prerequisite to evaluation (Rule 4: Principle of Order). It is true that a synthesis can and should be evaluated, but without specificity of evaluation (a judgement), it is difficult to achieve. Inasmuch as evaluation is normally a judgement based on an application, evaluation should logically follow Application.

Bloom's et al. subcategories of 6.10 *Judgements in terms of internal evidence* and 6.20 *Judgements in terms of external evidence* do not meet the criteria of being mutually exclusive (Rule 3). These subcategories tend to focus on the types of evidence rather than intellectual abilities and skills related to evaluation. See Table B: Summary of Taxonomic Rule Violations.

When evaluation and synthesis are expanded into subcategories of intellectual abilities and skills, it becomes clear that analysis is a sub-part of evaluation and that synthesis is independent of evaluation and not a prerequisite to evaluation. An evaluation of a synthesis is largely a reassessment or refinement. To reach a synthesis requires an evaluation to give cause for and direction to the synthesis.

Evaluation is seen as the major 4.0 objective with sub-categories of analysis and qualification. Evaluations typically deal with the degree or value of something in relation to some standards or criteria. Evaluation requires reflective, critical thinking and decision making. Therefore, 4.0 Evaluation has been redefined as: ability to analyze and qualify information or situations to make judgements.

4.1 Analysis

An analysis is the breaking down of a whole into its parts to discern how the parts are related to each other and how the parts are related to the whole.

An analysis tends to identify the characteristics and quantitative dimensions of information/content in a given context.

Bloom's et al. 4.00 *Analysis* focuses on the types of items one may analyze rather than on the intellectual abilities and skills of analysis. Bloom's et al. 4.10 *Analysis of elements*, 4.20 *Analysis of relationships*, and 4.30 *Analysis of organizational principles* do not meet the criteria of Rule 3: Mutually Exclusive and are vague as to any intellectual ability or skill. In the redefined taxonomy, Analysis (4.1) replaces Bloom's 6.10 *Judgements in terms of internal evidence* to better serve the evaluation process and communicate the intent of the objective (Rule 5).

As analysis is a subcategory of evaluation it should be within the same category. One would not perform an analysis for the sake of analysis. An analysis is usually performed as a first step in making a reasoned judgement. Facts and figures are gathered and sorted out. The interrelationship of the facts is discerned. A statement is made about the relationship, e.g., causes and effects, magnitudes, norms, deviations, percentages, and patterns of phenomena. During and/or after an analysis, tentative judgements are often made, either informally or formally, which indicate what the analysis has revealed. This is part of the critical thinking process. A detailed, lengthy analysis may reveal many findings. These are usually summarized or condensed into more manageable generalizations or summaries. Generalizations and summaries are not syntheses. They do not contain new arrangements or a new plan or communication.

4.2 Qualification

Whereas an analysis tends to identify the characteristics and quantitative dimensions of information/content in a given context, qualification determines the value, or the degree of deviation, or the degree of acceptance in relation to some criteria or standard. Thus, following an analysis, findings are qualified and a statement is made as to the value of the findings. This requires reflective thinking. Evidence is weighed in relation to what is, or ought to be--a value, criterion, or standard. Teachers, for example, do this in the process of arriving at grades for student work. Teachers assess the adequacy, strength, or relevance of the evidence, weigh it against the criteria, and determine a grade. Qualification may be as simple as a nod of the head in approval or as complex as a court of law. Together, analysis and qualification serve as a basis for making an evaluation and a judgement. 4.2 Qualification replaces Bloom's et al. 6.20 *Judgements in terms of external evidence* to better serve the evaluation process and communicate the intent of the objective (Rule 5). See Table 3F: Evaluation.

An example of the *evaluation* process is the methodology used in the evaluation of the various categories of the redefined taxonomies. The categories and subcategories are first *analyzed*. The components of each category are examined as to their definition, function and content. The components are then examined in relation to criteria (rules) to see if they *qualify*. Categories and content that do not meet the criteria are noted. The problem of what to do about the categories that are disqualified leads to the next level--synthesis.

Table 3F
Evaluation (Redefined)

4.0 Evaluation. Ability to analyze and qualify information and data or situations to make a judgement.

    4.1 **Analysis.** Ability to break down objects or ideas into simpler parts and see how the parts are related and organized (e.g., identification of ideas and components; determination of magnitudes, norms, deviations, percentages; determination of internal effects of components; determination of causes and effects; identification of patterns or processes).

        Applicable test descriptors: analyzes, quantifies, breaks down, separates, determines, identifies causes/effects, distinguishes, diagnoses.

    4.2 **Qualification**. Ability to discern a variance in measuring information against a criterion or standard that ought to be complied with, (i.e., identification of a value, criterion, or standard; comparison of evidence against the standard; identification of discrepancies).

        Applicable test descriptors: discriminates, compares, discerns, distinguishes, reconciles, juxtaposes, moralizes, rationalizes, qualifies, predicts, concludes, critiques, justifies, deduces.

5.0 Synthesis

Any discrepancies found during the evaluation process require resolution. Synthesis requires problem solving at a high level, i.e., proposing solutions to problems that may include multiple questions and factors. This generally requires a new or different arrangement of the components to form a new whole. Thus, following an evaluation, it is necessary to intellectually come up with remedies, answers, prescriptions, plans, innovations, or inventions, to resolve the problem and improve the situation. This is a critical thinking, creative thinking, problem solving process which may require innovative thinking. Good descriptors for this category are: new, different, modified, creative, innovative, and inventive.

Synthesis is seen as the highest and most difficult level of objective. Synthesis requires that the known information/content be evaluated (analyzed and qualified), and statements made as to what should be done through hypothesis and resolution. Synthesis may include creative, divergent, reflective, and problem solving thinking. Synthesis is redefined as: ability to hypothesize and resolve complex problems which yield new arrangements and answers. These answers are usually embodied in a set of plans and/or communications.

5.1 Hypothesis

A hypothesis is a tentative assumption made in order to draw out or test logical or empirical consequences. It can be described as a *good guess* based on theory and provides the basis for predicting outcomes. It is an interpretation of a practical situation or condition taken as the basis for action. According to Gay (1987, 544) a hypothesis is a tentative, reasonable, testable explanation for certain behaviors, phenomena, or events. She says there are two kinds of hypotheses, inductive and deductive. Inductive hypothesis is a generalization based observations. Deductive hypothesis is derived from a theory or evidence which supports, expands, or contradicts a theory. Thus, hypotheses range from best guesses to formalized hypotheses as we find them in research theses and dissertations. Hypothesizing requires critical and reflective thinking.

5.2 Resolution

A resolution, as defined here, is an answer to a complex problem. Resolution is the final stage of a deductive process combining thesis and antithesis into a new whole. The evaluation of complex problems may involve attention to multiple factors to satisfy the condition. A resolution is usually a conclusion reached after critical study or reflection, and entails a plan and/or a communication. Resolutions are based on multiple questions, facts, findings, evidence, and answers, and introduce new or different alternatives and perspectives, which, in turn, may be re-evaluated and refined before being implemented. A resolution usually involves deductive reasoning from a governing principle to the particular effects.

An example of a *synthesis* process is the synthesis of the various categories of the redefined taxonomies. The categories were evaluated and some were found wanting. Various terms were *hypothesized* to meet the taxonomic criteria. Terms of the categories were defined, examined and tested as *resolutions* to the problem. This cyclical process of analysis, qualification, hypothesis, and resolution resulted in the categories finally set forth in the 5.0 Synthesis category.

Synthesis can also be applied at an institutional or macro level. For example, in NCATE accreditation (National Council for the Accreditation of Teacher Education), all evidence related to the standards is analyzed. Based on the analysis and qualification of the evidence provided, an evaluation is made to determine the extent to which the standards are met. The judgement decisions are: 1) standard met, 2) standard met with minor weakness, and 3) standard not met. The judgement is communicated to the institution along with any cited weaknesses. The institution then must determine what must be done and how it will meet the unmet standards and overcome the weaknesses. This is a synthesis objective for the institution.

Table 3G
Synthesis (Redefined)

5.0 Synthesis. Ability to hypothesize and resolve complex problems which yield new arrangements or answers.

    5.1 **Hypothesis**. Ability to make tentative assumptions in order to draw out or test logical or empirical consequences (e.g., make assumptions and predictions, formulate a new hypothesis, speculate on a new treatment, investigate an idea).

    Applicable test descriptors: hypothesizes, projects, forecasts, assumes, speculates, prognosticates, predicts, theorizes, experiments, investigates.

    5.2 **Resolution**. Ability to answer complex problems (e.g., rearrange often diverse conceptions into a new whole, reach a conclusion after critical study or reflection, reason deductively from principle to particular effects, develop plans and communications).

    Applicable test descriptors: plans, solves, innovates, creates, invents, prescribes, devises, reconstructs, revises, rewrites, redefines.

The institution must determine (hypothesize, make assumptions) what must be done, what changes must be made, what needs to be developed, redefined, modified, generated, invented, etc., and develop a plan of action to overcome the weaknesses and meet the standard(s).

The processes of evaluation and synthesis are cyclically spiral. When the new ideas, prescriptions, innovations, etc., have been reliably and successfully implemented and evaluated (analyzed and qualified), they then become part of accepted knowledge and practice, providing no further refinement of the synthesis is needed. This cycle constitutes the ongoing process of change, growth and development, rational thought processes, critical thinking, reflective thinking, and problem solving thinking. See Table 3G: Synthesis.

Taxonomic Terminology

According to Rule 1 Applicability, the terms used must be expressible as gerund nouns. It is also useful to see how the terms are expressed as learning outcomes. It is useful for teachers to be able to recognize and classify intellectual abilities and skills when they observe that students are using them. It is also useful to be able to classify the results of their students abilities as learning outcomes. Table 3H: Reference List of Taxonomic Terminology and Derivations shows these terminological distinctions.

Summary

A set of definitions and new criteria and conditions for developing a taxonomy are first established as external criteria. Bloom's et al. taxonomy of cognitive objectives are critically evaluated (analyzed and qualified) as per the taxonomic rules and a redefined (synthesized) taxonomy that more accurately identifies and reflects intellectual abilities and skills is developed. *Knowledge* is reclassified in the taxonomy and placed as an information/ content input. The first category is posited as Conceptualization and includes subcategories of identification, definition, and generalization. The Comprehension category is accepted as meeting the taxonomic criteria. The Application category is expanded to include clarification and solution. The Analysis, Synthesis, and Evaluation categories are redefined and rearranged. Evaluation is redefined to include subcategories of analysis and qualification and is placed after Application. Synthesis is redefined to include hypothesis and resolution and placed as the highest order of objective. A redefined taxonomy is posited as in Table 3I: Redefined Taxonomy of Educational

Objectives: Cognitive Domain.

Throughout this restructuring, a greater specificity of intellectual abilities and skills is provided. Thinking abilities and skills, namely; critical thinking, reflective thinking, and problem solving thinking, is also facilitated.

Table 3H
Reference List of Taxonomic Terminology and Derivatives

Nouns	Gerund Nouns	Outcomes
1.0 Conceptualization	Conceptualizing	Conceptualizes
1.1 Identification	Identifying	Identifies
1.2 Definition	Defining	Defines
1.3 Generalization	Generalizing	Generalizes
2.0 Comprehension	Comprehending	Comprehends
2.1 Translation	Translating	Translates
2.2 Interpretation	Interpreting	Interprets
2.3 Extrapolation	Extrapolating	Extrapolates
3.0 Application	Applying	Applies
3.1 Clarification	Clarifying	Clarifies
3.2 Solution	Solving	Solves
4.0 Evaluation	Evaluating	Evaluates
4.1 Analysis	Analyzing	Analyzes
4.2 Qualification	Qualifying	Qualifies
5.0 Synthesis	Synthesizing	Synthesizes
5.1 Hypothesis	Hypothesizing	Hypothesizes
5.2 Resolution	Resolving	Resolves

Table 3I
Redefined Taxonomy of Educational Objectives: Cognitive Domain

---

Intellectual Abilities and Skills

1.0 Conceptualization. Ability to identify, define, and generalize an idea in a specific context.

    1.1 **Identification.** Ability to associate, remember and recall specific signs and symbols in relation to ideas, objects, or phenomena in a given context (e.g., name the sunshine state, identify the arm bones, state the primary colors, list the steps in a process, label an item, identify an acronym, recognize a body gesture).
    Applicable test descriptors: identifies, names, states, labels, lists, relates, recognizes.

    1.2 **Definition**. Ability to discern the essential qualities, limits, and meaning of a concept (e.g., define a term--outline, state the characteristics of a phenomena--electricity).
    Applicable test descriptors: defines, relates, states, matches.

    1.3 **Generalization**. Ability to integrate the particulars of an idea, object, or phenomena in order to be able to communicate the overall composition and nature of the concept (e.g., describe an object--mirror, explain a term--switch, outline a process).
    Applicable test descriptors: describes, reproduces, outlines, writes, explains, generalizes.

2.0 Comprehension. Ability to translate and interpret ideas, and extrapolate content information.

    2.1 **Translation**. Ability to put communication into another form (e.g., state problems in own words, read a musical score, translate words and phrases from a foreign language, describe a diagram/drawing, relate the meaning of a cartoon).
    Applicable test descriptors: converts, translates, draws, diagrams, relates, describes.

    2.2 **Interpretation**. Ability to explain ideas and interrelationships (e.g., give your own interpretation of an event, write a report explaining a set of data, explain a blueprint, represent by means of art).
    Applicable test descriptors: gives examples, paraphrases, explains, interprets, represents, tells.

Table 3I (Continued)

2.3   **Extrapolation**. Ability to make inferences from given information (e.g., make a forecast from a given set of data, project what is needed to meet an objective, identify a trend, derive a principle).
Applicable test descriptors: infers, projects, predicts, forecasts, estimates, extrapolates, derives, deduces.

3.0 Application. Ability to clarify a problem or situation and use appropriate principles and procedures to solve a specific problem or situation.

3.1   **Clarification**. Ability to isolate the elements of a singular problem or situation from its surrounding context (e.g., discern the relevant and nonrelevant elements, identify the specifics of the problem, define the problem).
Applicable test descriptors: identifies, discerns, defines, clarifies, isolates, diagnoses.

3.2   **Solution**. Ability to use appropriate principles and procedures in the solution of a specific problem or situation. (e.g., use math and accounting principles to balance a checkbook, use Ohm's law to compute voltage or amperage or resistance, use grammar rules to write sentences and paragraphs, use orthographic principles and procedures to construct a drawing, use the scientific process to do an experiment).
Applicable test descriptors: determines, decides, resolves, solves, shows, produces, uses, experiments.

4.0 Evaluation. Ability to analyze and qualify information and data or situations to make a judgement.

4.1   **Analysis**. Ability to break down objects or ideas into simpler parts and see how the parts are related and organized (e.g., identification of ideas and components; determination of magnitudes, norms, deviations, percentages; determination of internal effects of component; determination of causes and effects; identification of patterns or processes).
Applicable test descriptors: analyzes, quantifies, breaks down, separates, determines, identifies causes/effects, distinguishes, selects, diagnoses.

Table 3I (Continued)

4.2 **Qualification**. Ability to discern a variance in measuring information against a criterion or standard that ought to be complied with, (i.e., identification of a value, criterion, or standard; comparison of evidence against the standard; identification of discrepancies).

Applicable test descriptors: discriminates, compares, discerns, distinguishes, reconciles, juxtaposes, moralizes, rationalizes, qualifies, predicts, concludes, critiques, justifies, deduces.

5.0 Synthesis. Ability to hypothesize and resolve complex problems which yield new arrangements or answers.

5.1 **Hypothesis**. Ability to make tentative assumptions in order to draw out or test logical or empirical consequences (e.g., make assumptions and predictions, formulate a new hypothesis, speculate on a new treatment, investigate an idea).

Applicable test descriptors: guesses, assumes, projects, hypothesizes, formulates, predicts, rationalizes, reconciles, speculates, prognosticates, theorizes, experiments, investigates.

5.2 **Resolution.** Ability to answer complex problems (e.g., rearrange diverse conceptions into a new whole; reach a conclusion after critical study or reflection; reason deductively from principle to particular effects; develop plans and communications).

Applicable test descriptors: plans, solves, innovates, creates, invents, prescribes, devises, reconstructs, revises, rewrites, redefines.

Questions to Consider

1. What is a taxonomy?
2. What are the differences between information, knowledge, and content?
3. Why is *conceptualization* used to replace *knowledge* in Bloom's et al. taxonomy?
4. Why is *knowledge* not an intellectual ability or skill?
5. How are concepts acquired?
6. In your own words, how would you explain the *comprehension* category?

7. Why was the *application* category expanded?
8. Why was *analysis* placed under the category of *evaluation*?
9. Why is *qualification* a subcategory of *evaluation*?
10. Do you agree or disagree that *synthesis* is not a prerequisite to *evaluation*? Why?
11. Are *hypothesis* and *resolution* reasonable subcategories of synthesis?
12. Select a lesson you teach. What would be the symbolic and descriptive inputs for the lesson?
13. How does the redefined cognitive domain reflect the ideas of constructivism?
14. What questions do you have?

References

1. Bloom, Benjamin S. (Ed.), Englehart, Max D., Furst, Edward J., Hill, Walker H. and Krathwohl, David R. 1956. *Taxonomy of educational objectives. The classification of educational goals, Handbook I: cognitive domain.* New York: Longmans, Green, Co.
2. Caine, Renate N. and Caine, Geoffrey C. 1997. *Education on the edge of possibility.* Alexandra, Virginia: Association for Supervision and Curriculum Development.
3. Gay, R. L. 1987. *Educational research, competencies for analysis and application.* Columbus, Ohio: Merrill Publishing Company, Third Edition.
4. Gronlund, Norman E. 1970. *Stating behavioral objectives for classroom instruction.* New York: Macmillan Publishing Co., Inc.
5. Mager, Robert F. *1984. Preparing instructional objectives.* Revised Second Edition. Belmont, California: Pitman Learning, Inc.
6. Marzano, Robert J., Brandt, Ronald S., Hughes, Carolyn S., Jones, Beau F., Presseisen, Barbara Z., Rankin, Stuart C., and Suhor, Charles. 1988. *Dimensions of thinking: A framework for curriculum and instruction.* Alexandria, Virginia: Association for Supervision and Curriculum Development.
7. Shepard, L. A. 1989. *Why we need better assessments.* Educational Leadership. 46, 7:4-9. April.
8. Woodruff, Asahel D. 1961. *Basic concepts of teaching.* Scranton, Pennsylvania: Chandler Publishing Co. Concise Edition.

Chapter 4

The Affective Domain: Redefined

Introduction

David B. Krathwohl, Benjamin S. Bloom, and Bertram B. Masia prepared the *Taxonomy of Educational Objectives. The Classification of Educational Goals, Handbook II: Affective Domain* (1964) to help teachers describe and achieve objectives pertaining to aspects of behavior that involve attitudes and values. The main categories in Krathwohl's et al. taxonomy are: receiving, responding, valuing, organization, and characterization. It is assumed that the reader has some familiarity with the affective taxonomy. If not, the reader should review the condensed version of the taxonomy of affective objectives presented in Appendix B.

Krathwohl's et al. affective domain deals with affective elements such as: interests, appreciations, attitudes, values, and adjustments to them (Krathwohl et al. 1964, 37). No content knowledge is specified as an input. It is assumed that affective dimensions will be taught along with cognitive knowledges as applicable. Since Krathwohl's et al. taxonomy has no particular content input, teachers have had little direction in implementing the objectives in the classroom.

The redefined taxonomy is viewed as a set of process objectives within a system of inputs, processes, and outputs. In the cognitive domain, *symbolic and descriptive* information/content are the primary inputs of emphasis to the process of developing cognitive abilities and skills.

Similarly, in the redefined affective domain, *symbolic and prescriptive and* information/content are the primary inputs of emphasis for the process objectives for students to become acculturated individuals. See Fig. 4.1 Instructional System for the Affective Domain.

The prescriptive content *inputs* are embodied in and derived from social/cultural and religious values, morals, customs, philosophies, theologies, and laws. This information/content input knowledge (others' knowledge) tends to prescribe *what ought to be*. The *process* objectives in the redefined taxonomy are posited as: receiving, responding, valuing,

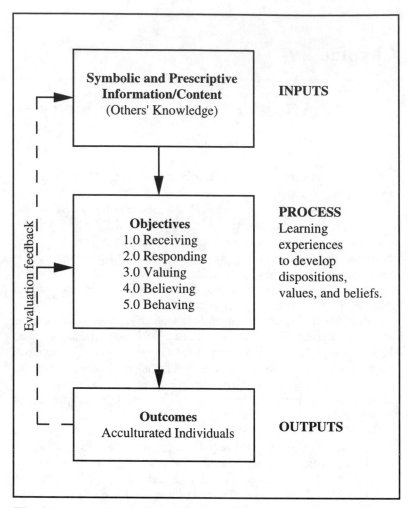

Fig. 4.1 Instructional System for the Affective Domain

Fig. 4.1 shows an instructional system for the affective domain with symbolic and prescriptive information/content (others' knowledge) as inputs to the process objectives of receiving, responding, valuing, believing, and behaving to produce outcomes of acculturated individuals. Evaluation feedback provides for adjustment of the information/content inputs and process objectives.

believing, and behaving. The composite effect of these content inputs and process objectives influence how a student is disposed to view and interact with the world, the school, the teacher, their peers, the content, classroom activities and situations. The *output* is seen as acculturated individuals with dispositions, values, beliefs conducive to a democratic society. These prescriptive values and beliefs are expressed in an individual's general feelings about aspects of life and dispositional responses to experiences. The teacher's job is to provide and facilitate learning situations which predispose and enable students to explore, reinforce, or change their prevailing dispositions, values, and beliefs.

Prescriptive inputs reflect the values, morals, beliefs, and philosophical principles of an individual and society. They represent a reflection of what is right and wrong, and what is good and true, and worth of various values. In the schools, and in the family, they are the means by which social democratic customs, values, and beliefs are passed on and instilled in the next generation. Collectively, these values become the foundation for responding to life's situations in a variety of contexts. These values and beliefs are exhibited in one's feelings about a situation and one's dispositional response to a situation. These dispositions make up and color one's character.

From many points of view, the affective domain may be equal to, if not more important, than the cognitive domain. When the affective domain is subordinated to the cognitive domain, the outcomes may fall short of the needs of the student. Gaining knowledge *is* important in school, however, the acquisition and development of feelings, values, and beliefs are equally important. When cognitive concepts, facts, principles, etc. are taught, it is important to include the *whys* and *wherefores*--the values and reasons associated with them. Since affective objectives are typically long term, and more difficult to measure than cognitive objectives, they tend to receive less emphasis in the curriculum. From the student's point of view, there is an affective dimension in every lesson. For example, at a very general level, students may feel ambivalent and apprehensive at the start of a lesson, but feel satisfied they have learned something new by the end of the lesson.

When the affective domain is neglected or ignored, we weaken the individual and consequently society in general. The result is a growing preponderance of negative social behaviors. For example, some individuals may lack moral and social values and have a disposition to lie, cheat, steal, maim, and murder. Many may have dispositions to be prejudiced, use ethnic slurs and stereotyping, and be racists. Others may have a lack of respect for the themselves, for others, and for authority.

Conversely, the affective domain is also critical to the development of lifelong interests, values, and appreciations, such as for art, music, reading, sports, hobbies, etc. Thus, it is important for teachers to provide learning experiences in which students can develop their own positive educational and social feelings, values and beliefs--their habits of mind.

The redefined affective domain deals with dispositions (prevailing tendencies) as related to prescriptive knowledge of society (cultural and religious morals, customs, theologies, philosophies, and laws). All behavior is influenced to some degree by knowledge of these social/cultural and religious prescriptions. The influence of this knowledge on the way one behaves is called a disposition. For example, if an individual holds love as a value, when the situation arises, the individual may be disposed to be kind, sympathetic, compassionate, affectionate, friendly, gentle, agreeable, or pleasant, depending on the circumstance.

The degree to which a student is acculturated with dispositions, (feelings, values, and beliefs) is dependent upon the degree to which prescriptive information/content is included in the curriculum and instruction related to the inputs. It is posited herein that it is essential to teach prescriptive knowledge to acculturate a student with the values and beliefs of the society in which he/she lives. It should not be a matter of happenstance for teachers to determine affective objectives related to the subjects they teach.

The redefined taxonomy focuses on the development of values and beliefs associated with prescriptive knowledge as well as other knowledge. A value is a concept of the relative worth, utility or importance of something. A value is something intrinsically worthwhile and desirable. Valuing (the behavior) is the disposition (prevailing tendency) to consider and assess the desirability, worth and validity of a value.

A student cannot be handed a value or disposition. Values and their associated feelings and responses are developed as the result of one's values and experiences with values. All a teacher can do, is to talk about values or set up role playing situations, or dilemmas to work with to try to influence the student to be *predisposed* toward what is being taught, i.e., to approach the situation with a certain *mind set*. Teachers can model values, and set up learning experiences which help students confront and develop values. Teachers try to help the students become predisposed, for example, to feel about or see situations in a certain way, to like/dislike some aspect of the subject, or want to take some action. After an initial experience, and if the student felt satisfied with the experience, the student may approach similar situations with the same disposition. It is through experiences that feelings and their dispositions are strengthened, weakened, or modified. It is important that teachers plan learning experiences which promote positive values and enable students to develop positive feelings and dispositions. Consistent dispositions, over time, may become a belief and a habit of mind.

In this redefinition, Krathwohl's et al. affective domain and categories are largely accepted in intent and spirit. Some terms have been changed and a few added to reflect a level of affective development and to comply with the taxonomic rules. The redefined categories of the taxonomy are: receiving, responding, valuing, believing, and behaving. See Table 4A: Abbreviated Taxonomy of Affective Objectives for a comparison of the two taxonomies. Believing replaces *organization*, and behaving replaces *characterization by value or value complex*. Teachers have difficulty with the abstract objectives such as *organization* and *characterization by value or value complex* in the classroom. Believing and behaving are more identifiable concrete objectives and behaviors and thus are more likely to receive emphasis in this important domain. These are higher level, long term objectives. If teachers cannot readily identify with such objectives, it is unlikely that they will receive the attention they deserve in the curriculum. An attempt is made herein to make affective behaviors and objectives more recognizable to teachers in the classroom.

As in the cognitive domain, one cannot see thinking abilities and skills, thus a student's knowledge can only be observed by their behavior or a product of behavior. Similarly, in the affective domain, we cannot see a students internal feelings, dispositions, values, and beliefs. These are only observable when they exhibit them in their behavior and demeanor. Thus, to be of service to teachers, the affective taxonomy needs to be expressed in behavioral terms. Examples of how teachers can facilitate the affective domain are included in the category descriptions to promote affective development.

Before proceeding with the discussion of the taxonomy, it will be useful to consider some definitions and review the common criteria for structuring a taxonomy.

Definitions

Taxonomy--a classification system that establishes the hierarchy of the parts to other parts and the parts to the whole. It is an orderly classification of things according to their presumed natural relationships. For example, in classifying dispositions, they would be classified according to their level of difficulty and complexity in the learning process.

Feeling--an often indefinite state of mind (a feeling of ambivalence in making a choice), also such a state with regard to something (a feeling of dislike) or a general emotional condition, sensibilities, the overall quality of one's awareness.

Feeling applies to any response or awareness marked by pain, pleasure, attraction, or repulsion. It may support the existence of a response without implying anything definite about its nature or intensity. *Emotion* implies a clearly defined feeling and usually greater excitement or agitation.

Table 4A
Abbreviated Taxonomy of Affective Objectives

Redefined Affective Taxonomy	Affective Taxonomy (Krathwohl et al. 1964)
Dispositions (prevailing tendencies)	
1.0 Receiving	**1.0 Receiving** (Attending)
1.1 Awareness	1.1 Awareness
1.2 Willingness	1.2 Willingness to receive
1.3 Attentiveness	1.3 Controlled or selected attention
2.0 Responding	**2.0 Responding**
2.1 Acquiescing	2.1 Acquiescence in responding
2.2 Complying	2.2 Willingness to respond
2.3 Assessing	2.3 Satisfaction in response
3.0 Valuing	**3.0 Valuing**
3.1 Accepting	3.1 Acceptance of a value
3.2 Preferring	3.2 Preference for a value
3.3 Confirming	3.3 Commitment
4.0 Believing	**4.0 Organization**
4.1 Trusting	4.1 Conceptualization of a value
4.2 Committing	4.2 Organization of a value system
5.0 Behaving	**5.0 Characterization by value or value complex**
5.1 Demonstrating	5.1 Generalized set
5.2 Modifying	5.2 Characterization

Disposition--a prevailing tendency, inclination, a natural attitude toward things. The tendency to act in a certain manner under given circumstances, a demeanor, customary mood and attitude toward the life around one. Relative enduring *habits of mind* or characteristic ways of responding to experience across types of situations.

Predisposition--to dispose in advance, make susceptible, to be inclined.

Value--the relative worth, utility, or importance of, something intrinsically valuable or desirable. Valuation--a judgement or appreciation of worth or character.

Belief--a state or habit of mind in which trust or confidence is placed in some person or thing, a tenet or body of tenets held by a group, a conviction of the truth of some statement or reality of a fact, especially when well grounded. To have a firm conviction as to the reality or goodness of something, to take as true or honest.

Inputs to the Affective Domain System

As stated in the introduction, the prescriptive content *inputs* of emphasis are embodied in and derived from social/cultural and religious values, morals, customs, philosophies, theologies, and laws. These information/ content knowledge inputs (others' knowledge) tend to prescribe *what ought to be*. The following are brief definitions of these inputs without regard to their classification as prescriptive knowledge inputs.

Morals. Morals are the principles of what is right and wrong in behavior. They conform to a standard of right behavior, i.e., what is virtuous, good, and fair.

Customs. Customs are the practices common to many or habitual to an individual. These are long established practices that may be considered as unwritten laws. These are the conventions that regulate social life, e.g., manners, etiquette, observance of events such as holidays, birthdays, weddings, etc.

Theologies. Theologies are the interpretations of religious faiths, practices, and experiences. Theologies deal with thoughts about God and God's relationship to the world. The Judeo-Christian theology, for example, provided the basic tenets of moral conduct and human rights for the Constitution and Bill of Rights, the basis of our laws and freedoms.

Philosophies. Philosophies deal with the study of the nature of knowledge and existence and the principle of moral and esthetics value. They deal with wisdom and insight as applied to life itself. *Ethics* is a branch of philosophy which deals with what is good, bad, and moral duty or obligation. They include the principles of good conduct governing an individual or group.

Laws. Laws are rules of conduct or action laid down and enforced by the supreme governing authority of a community or society. They are a collection of customs and rules. Laws deal with the principles that govern actions or procedures, obligation, and obedience.

When descriptive (what was, is, will be) and symbolic content is being taught it is also important to teach the prescriptive information/content (what ought to be) dimensions as well. Prescriptive content can also be taught separately as subject matter. Schools should be teaching the values of social/cultural customs, morals, beliefs, ethics, and laws in order that students become encouraged to adapt to the culture and society in which they live.

Taxonomic Criteria/Conditions

A taxonomy is a classification system which establishes the hierarchy of the parts to other parts and parts to the whole. The taxonomy is described as a hierarchy because, for example, responding relies on prior reception, and is a prerequisite to valuing. In constructing or evaluating a taxonomy, it is useful to have some common taxonomic criteria and conditions against which the taxonomy can be judged. These requisites are listed here as *rules*.

Rule 1. The taxonomy must have *applicability,* e.g., be relevant for the function for which it will be used. When the taxonomy is used to classify overt behaviors and products of behavior reflecting dispositions, values and beliefs and their feelings, the terms used in the categories and subcategories must *be able to be expressed* as verbs or gerund nouns (words ending in *ing*). A test for this is, for example, to add *ing* to the terms, thus, receiving, responding, valuing, etc., or organization--organizing, characterization--characterizing.

Rule 2. The taxonomy, as a whole, must be *totally inclusive*--the components represent all categories in a given context, e.g., feelings, dispositions, values, and beliefs. The categories must be comprehensive. There should be no error of omission among the parts or between the parts and the whole. As a test, there should nothing you can think of (any behavior exhibiting a disposition) that would not be able to be classified under one of the categories or subcategories.

Rule 3. The categories of the taxonomy must be *mutually exclusive*--there is no overlap between categories or within subcategories of a category. Each category stands independent from the other categories in intent and function. As a test, the subcategories are explicit enough to give definition to the category and the terms used are not repeated within a category. A subterm in one category can be used in another category, but not within the same category. As a principle, it is better not to repeat a term in a category to avoid confusion.

Rule 4. The categories must be arranged following a consistent *principle of order*--e.g., from simple to complex, easy to difficult, concrete to abstract, prerequisite to requisite, cause-effect, etc. If a category is subdivided it must have at least two subcategories which also follow the same principle of order.

Rule 5. The *terms* used to identify categories and subcategories should *communicate* the idea and be representative of those used in the field. A test for this is *Do the generic terms communicate the intent of the objectives to teachers in the field?*

Coding and Process

The major categories may be called first order objectives and can be designated as 1.0, 2.0, 3.0, etc. A subcategory within any first order category may be called a second order objective, e.g., 2.0--2.1, 2.2, 2.3, etc. Further breakdown within an order would be coded with its place and fit within the taxonomy, e.g., 2.1--2.1.1, 2.1.2, 2.1.3, etc., 2.2--2.2.1, 2.2.2, 2.2.3, etc.

In developing the second order of objectives, the same Rules 1-5 apply. For example, 2.0 Responding, (is now the whole) and any sub-orders established must have applicability, be totally inclusive of responding, mutually exclusive to each other, be arranged following a consistent principle of order, and communicate the intent. The same procedure and criteria are used for any third order classification of behavior. The coding, criteria and process would continue ad infinitum.

Redefined Taxonomy of Affective Objectives

The following are classifications of dispositions (prevailing tendencies), which range from low level and low intensities to higher level and stronger intensities. The composite effects of these dispositions influence how an individual views and interacts with the world, the school, the teacher, their peers, classroom activities and situations. These influences are described here as dispositions. The dispositions are placed on the positive side of the pain/pleasure continuum, as opposed to its negative side. See Table 2B: Prescriptive Knowledge (Truth) Continuum.

1.0 Receiving.

In this redefined taxonomy, receiving is defined as being aware, willing, and attentive. The general goal of receiving is to produce in the student a willingness to receive and attend to certain stimuli. This is the lowest level of interest and is a very passive activity for the student. It is the starting point of the learning process for the student. Receiving is concerned with sensitizing learners to certain stimuli and phenomena, and enabling them to become more focused in their attention to what is being taught. This becomes their *set* for the lesson.

At this initial starting point, little overt behavior can be discerned, thus *ing* words seldom apply (violation of Rule 1). The task of the teacher is to be active in getting, holding, and directing the attention of the student. The suffix *ness* used in the second order objectives denotes a *state of being*, a condition or a quality. The terms awareness, willingness, and attentiveness indicate this passivity. Taken collectively, these three second order objectives meet the criteria of Rule 1: Applicability.

Because of the passive nature of receiving, it is seldom worthwhile for a teacher to test their students for receiving dispositions. Test descriptors for receiving are mainly in terms of sensing, listening, seeing, paying attention, etc. However, receiving is an essential prerequisite to responding.

1.1 Awareness.

Awareness means a disposition to be conscious of life around one. Students come to the learning situation with all of their dispositions, knowledge, and experience and it is up to the teacher to get them in a state of readiness to learn and focus their attention on the lesson. Awareness means they are in a current state of consciousness in their normal environment. They know where they are and what's going on around them. They are aware of the approximate time of day. They are aware of their own feelings. They take into account a situation, phenomenon, or state of affairs. They have some awareness in factors such as dress, furnishings, temperature, and architecture in their surrounding environment. They can differentiate the sights and sounds in the school. They are sensitive to the social situations around them. Their current disposition may be positive, neutral, or negative ranging between happy/unhappy, friendly/unfriendly, pleasant/quarrelsome, etc.

The intent of the teacher should be to establish and promote a positive and conducive learning environment for the student and a general feeling of comfort and security.

Teachers can facilitate awareness as a predisposition by maintaining a pleasant or pleasurable learning environment reflecting the characteristics of what they teach, e.g., related objects and equipment around the room, bulletin or display boards, visual aids, etc. This provides instant recognition of atmosphere of a learning environment. Teachers facilitate awareness in the classroom by establishing rules and routines, e.g., when the class is seated, the teacher calls for attention, takes attendance, and begins the lesson. This provides an aura of general expectation for order.

1.2 Willingness

Willingness means a feeling about and a disposition to choose to tolerate and consider certain experiences rather than ignoring or rejecting them. It may involve neutrality or suspended judgement toward the stimulus. The student is willing to take notice of a phenomenon and give his/her attention. The student finds some attraction or interest in the stimuli. It is a condition in which the student is inclined to feel he/she is not opposed. Certain stimuli may be favored or preferred over other stimuli.

Teachers facilitate willingness as a predisposition in their *lesson initiating* behavior or *set*. It is up to the teacher to move students to a positive state of being, to get them interested and motivated. The intent here is to make students more focused, to get their attention, to get them to listen carefully, to watch, observe, and be alert.

The teacher's activity is directed at motivating, gaining, and keeping their students' attention and interest so that they will be willing to receive information. Teachers also facilitate willingness by using a pleasant, nonthreatening voice, by accepting students as they are, caring about the student, by positive gestures, complimenting students, being cheerful rather than disgruntled, and so forth. Teachers try to interest students and stimulate curiosity by telling a short pointed story, drawing on the board, wearing a costume, giving a short demonstration, asking a pointed question, or manipulating a related object.

1.3 Attentiveness.

Attentiveness means a feeling about and a disposition to attend to certain experiences despite the presence of distracting stimuli. This means students are attracted enough to be inclined to pay attention to what is being said or done. Students should not be looking out the window to see what is going on outside, but should be listening carefully to what is being said and closely observing what is being shown or done.

Teachers facilitate attentiveness as a predisposition by the ways in which they present information, by means of interesting activities, calling students by name, by interacting with the students, posing thought provoking questions, varying their teaching techniques, and by using interesting books and other teaching materials. See Table 4B: Receiving.

Table 4B
Receiving (Redefined)

1.0   Receiving. Disposition to be aware, willing, and attentive.

   1.1   **Awareness**. Disposition to be conscious of life around one (e.g., being aware of the surrounding environment, perceives different styles of dress, hears different classroom noises, knows the approximate time of day, is conscience of the attitudes of others).
   Applicable test descriptors: senses, sees, listens, perceives, is aware.

   1.2   **Willingness**. Disposition to choose to tolerate and consider certain experiences rather than ignoring or rejecting them (e.g., listen to specific types of music, listens to the views of others without interrupting, open to watching a film, listens to different points of view).
   Applicable test descriptors: offers, watches, listens, tolerates, is willing, chooses, eagerness.

   1.3   **Attentiveness**. Disposition to attend to certain experiences despite distracting stimuli (e.g., pays attention to what is being said, observes a demonstration, concentrates on the lyrics of a song, listens carefully to a poem, is alert to a potential danger).
   Applicable test descriptors: observes, concentrates, attends, is interested, is focused.

2.0 Responding.

In the redefined taxonomy, responding is defined as a disposition to acquiesce, comply with, and assess a response situation. The intent of this category is to enable the student to become attracted or interested enough to respond to a stimulus and assess their feelings about it. Compliance and assessment are good descriptors of this category. It includes: acquiescing--a disposition to accept the ideas and responsibilities suggested by others as being worthwhile, complying--a disposition to act with little or no prompting, and assessing--a disposition to appraise one's feelings about a response.

2.1 Acquiescing.

Acquiescing means a disposition to accept ideas, and actions and responsibilities suggested by others as worthwhile. The student basically finds nothing distasteful or unsatisfactory about an idea and accepts it. Krathwohl's et al. 2.1 *Acquiescence in responding* is acceptable in intent, but violates Rule 1: Applicability. Acquiescence needs to be expressed as acquiescing for consistency.

Teachers facilitate acquiescence as a predisposition by having students discuss why an idea is good or not so good, the benefits and detriments, or what an object does and why it may be useful. Teachers can promote and motivate students toward the importance of understanding ideas, objects, and phenomena, social situations, etc., and the need for: accurateness, thoroughness, respectfulness, politeness, helpfulness, fairness, neatness, carefulness, safety consciousness or safeness, etc.

2.2 Complying.

Complying means a disposition to act with little or no prompting. Complying means the student chooses to or is motivated to respond. Teachers can readily see that students comply as opposed to being willing to respond. The student's curiosity or interest is aroused to the point where he/she wants to or is motivated to give a response. The new motivations are close enough to prior experiences that the student feels no fear in making a response. Students may be aroused to the point where they feel they to want to ask a question, make a statement, give an opinion, or take an action.

When contact with subject matter is followed by positive consequences, the subject will tend to become a stimulus for an approach response. Conversely, whenever contact with subject matter is followed by aversive consequences, the subject may become a stimulus for an avoidance response. Whenever experience with a subject is followed by a positive (pleasant) consequence, the probability is increased that the subject will be approached again in the future. Students may be motivated and disposed to follow directions, do homework assignments, cooperate with others, observe

Table 4C
Summary of Taxonomic Rule Violations

Taxonomic Rules	Krathwohl's Taxonomy: Affective Objectives	Rule Violations
Rule 1 **Applicability** Relevant to function. Gerund noun.	**1.0 Receiving** (Attending) 1.1 Awareness 1.2 Willingness to receive 1.3 Controlled or selected attention	**1.0 Receiving** #5. No direct violation, but communication needs to be improved.
Rule 2 **Total inclusiveness** Represents all categories in a given context.	**2.0 Responding** 2.1 Acquiescence in responding 2.2 Willingness to respond 2.3 Satisfaction in response	**2.0 Responding** #1 and 5. No direct violation, but terms and communication needs to be improved. #3. 2.2 and 1.2 are in conflict.
Rule 3 **Mutual exclusiveness** No overlap between categories or within subcategories.	**3.0 Valuing** 3.1 Acceptance of a value 3.2 Preference for a value 3.3 Commitment	**3.0 Valuing** #4. Commitment is better placed under a higher level. #5. Confirming replaces commitment.
Rule 4 **Principle of order** e.g., Simple to complex. Prerequisite to requisite. Must have at least 2 subcategories.	**4.0 Organization** 4.1 Conceptualization of a value 4.2 Organization of a value system	**4.0 Organization** #4. Conceptualization is out of order with 3.3 commitment. #1 and #5. Communication needs to be improved. Organization of a value system is not a recognizable behavior.
Rule 5 **Communicate intent** Identifiable behavior in the classroom.	**5.0 Characterization by value or value complex** 5.1 Generalized set 5.2 Characterization	**5.0 Characterization by value or value complex** #5. Communicattion needs to be improved. #1. Generalized set and characterization are not gerund nouns.

safety precautions, and obey traffic signals.

Teachers can recognize compliance as a disposition by students raising their hands, making statements or giving opinions, following directions, and doing what was requested. Teachers can facilitate compliance by praising students for their responses, calling on them by name, and by elaborating on student responses. Teachers can praise students for their honesty, accuracy, correctness, helpfulness, politeness, open-mindedness, constraint, etc. When students are praised for their behavior, they are more likely to be disposed to repeat the compliance behavior which earned them recognition.

Complying is substituted for Krathwohl's et al. 2.2 *Willingness to respond* category (Rule 5, Communicate the intent). In addition, since Krathwohl's et al. 1.2 Willingness to receive uses *willingness*, it is in violation of Rule 3, Mutually exclusive. See Table 4C: Summary of Taxonomic Rule Violations.

2.3 Assessing.

Assessing means a disposition to appraise one's feelings about what was received and one's response to it. It is hoped the student will feel satisfaction in his/her response. However, some may have an aversive reaction, a feeling of concern or frustration, while others may be neutral with no particular feeling, one way or the other. Signs of nonverbal response assessments include, for example, being excited in what they are doing, feeling pleased with their responses, seeking enjoyable activities, reading beyond the assignment for enjoyment, enjoying helping others, complying with directions, participating in activities, and observing classroom rules. Signs of verbal appraisals include, for example, stating that they liked/disliked aspects of something, want to or do not want to do something, felt something was easy or hard, felt sure or unsure about something.

Teachers facilitate assessment as a predisposition by asking student how they felt about a learning experience. Did they feel a sense of satisfaction? Did they like/dislike an activity? Why did they like/dislike the activity? Did they feel they learned something? Why didn't they feel satisfied or like the experience? Ongoing self-assessment of feelings and their dispositions provide important feedback to the student and teacher so adjustments can be made in teaching and learning. Teachers also facilitate a disposition to positive assessing by positive reinforcement, praising students for their responses, or a pat on the back and a good word. Teachers need to find something good to say about each student sometime during the lesson, e.g., comment on his/her accuracy in math, spelling, etc., his/her helpfulness in assisting others, his/her observation of safety precautions, his/her attentiveness, politeness, and achievement. See Table 4D: Responding.

Table 4D
Responding (Redefined)

2.0 **Responding**. Disposition to acquiesce, comply with, and assess a response situation.

    2.1 **Acquiescing**. Disposition to accept ideas, actions and responsibilities suggested by others as worthwhile (e.g., sees the need to complete homework assignments, accepts another person's idea, agrees to participate in an activity, allows another person to hold one's hand).

    Applicable test descriptors: acquiesces, accepts, agrees, allows.

    2.2 **Complying**. Disposition to act with little or no prompting (e.g., helps others without prompting, participates in activities, observes classroom rules, follows directions, practices music lessons without prompting, volunteers to do a task).

    Applicable test descriptors: agrees, complies, observes, follows, obeys, conforms, cooperates, volunteers.

    2.3 **Assessing.** Disposition to appraise one's feelings about a response (e.g., felt uneasy about reading aloud, enjoyed participating in a group activity, wants to do more, is interested in something, enjoyed singing).

    Applicable test descriptors: likes/dislikes, wants to/does not want to, enjoys, is interested/uninterested, felt activity was easy/hard, was satisfied/unsatisfied, is sure/unsure, is ambivalent.

3.0 Valuing.

In the redefined taxonomy, Krathwohl's et al. 3.1 *Acceptance of a value* and 3.2 *Preference for a value* are acceptable in meeting the criteria in intent, but need to be replaced by accepting and preferring to be mutually exclusive (Rule 3). Both terms relate to a value. To be consistent, the terms should be accepting and preferring.

Valuing is defined as a disposition to accept, prefer, and confirm a value. Valuing is expressing an opinion about a value or worth of something. It includes: accepting--a disposition to endorse a basic value, preferring--a disposition to discriminate among values, and confirming--a disposition to verify the worth of a value through rationalization or experience.

Confirming means a disposition to verify the worth of a value through rationalization or experience. Confirming replaces Krathwohl's et al. 3.3 *Commitment* for it is through experience that feelings and dispositions for certain values may be examined, strengthened or weakened, confirmed and changed. The student may or may not commit to a value. A students' experience need not be a commitment per se, but the experience may confirm a students' disposition about the worth of an experience. Thus, 3.3 *Commitment* does not meet the criteria of Rule 1: Applicability and Rule 5: Communication of intent. See Table 4C: Summary of Taxonomic Rule Violations. Krathwohl's et al. *Commitment* as a subcategory is reclassified in the redefined taxonomy under 4.0 Believing as a sub-objective.

3.1 Accepting.

Accepting means a disposition to endorse a basic value. Accepting means agreeing with a basic proposition or assumption. This is largely intellectualizing an idea or value and finding it of worth, agreeing that it has merit, and having the feeling that the idea may be trusted.

Teachers can predispose students to acceptance by having students explain, compare and contrast points of view and by asking students why they like or dislike, approve or disapprove, agree or disagree that something is good or bad. Teachers can also help students be predisposed toward a value by having students express their views and opinions about a value, e.g., self-discipline, responsibility, integrity, honesty, patriotism, loyalty, freedom, human rights, democracy, cleanliness, health, respect, dignity, friendliness, trust, love, conservation, beauty, chastity, individualism, patience, and courtesy, to name a few.

3.2 Preferring.

Preferring means a disposition to discriminate among alternative values. Preferring a value means expressing a willingness to choose and be identified with a value. When given a choice, one alternative is favored or selected over another because it is perceived as having more desirable and valuable qualities. Preference shows a more positive feeling about and a disposition to choose an alternative satisfying to the student.

Teachers can predispose students to preferences by having students compare and contrast different points of view, explaining why one thing or idea may be better than another, and by considering possible consequences.

3.3 *Confirming.*

Confirming means a disposition to verify the worth of a value through rationalization or experience. It is the testing out of a value preference or strongly held opinion through deduction or experience and validating that it has worth. It is the resultant sense that a value or set of values is worthwhile and should be observed when the same or a similar situation is encountered.

Table 4E
Valuing (Redefined)

3.0 Valuing. Disposition to accept, prefer, and confirm a value.
    3.1 **Accepting**. Disposition to endorse a basic value (e.g., agrees sports are worthwhile, endorses healthful lifestyles, endorses democratic principles, rejects violence, accepts peaceful means for settling disputes, endorses truthfulness, opposes deceit).
    Applicable test descriptors: accepts, agrees, endorses, selects, rejects, opposes.
    3.2 **Preferring**. Disposition to discriminate among alternative values (e.g., when given a choice situation: thinks one should be honest, thinks one should not use drugs, feels one should help other, feels one should not prejudge others, favors a democratic process, chooses nonviolence, supports chastity).
    Applicable test descriptors: favors, selects, prefers, supports, chooses, compares, discriminates.
    3.3 **Confirming**. Disposition to verify the worth of a value through experience (e.g., after an experience: feels good about helping someone, sees that patience is a virtue, sees that personal relations are better when one respects the others' opinions, finds satisfaction in cooperating with others, sees merit in being courteous).
    Applicable test descriptors: verifies, concludes, rationalizes, tests, justifies, supports, validates, confirms, judges, is disposed to should/should not, would/would not.

Teachers can facilitate confirmation as a disposition by setting up lesson experiences and activities which enable students to intellectually explore, reinforce, or change values, by having students see for themselves, by describing the result of an applied value, and by asking students how they felt after having done or said something. Results of confirming lead to feelings and dispositions in students ranging between aspects of likes/dislikes, would/would not, agreeing/disagreeing, should/should not, want/does not want, interested/not interested, etc. See Table 4E: Valuing.

4.0 Believing.

The intent of this category is the establishment of a beginning belief. Believing involves trusting and committing to a value(s) as a guiding principle. Believing includes: trusting--a disposition to have confidence in and rely on a value as a guiding principle, and committing--a disposition to internalize and adhere to a value as a guiding principle.

Beliefs are rooted in values. Beliefs are trusted values, i.e., guiding principles. A belief is a habit of mind in which trust or confidence is placed in some person, idea, object, or situation. It includes a tenet or body of tenets held by a group. It is conviction of the truth of some statement or reality of a fact, especially when well grounded. To believe, is to have a firm conviction as to the reality or goodness of something, to take something as true or honest. A belief has to do with the degree or strength or trustworthiness of a value or set of values, a faith in something. For example, one may trust and believe that $a^2 + b^2 = c^2$, or $E = IR$, or trust the moral principle that honesty is the best policy or believe in freedom and justice.

Sets of values are organized into a belief. Trust in a value or tenet is established by the consistency that a certain value principle is felt and found to be true and good, (e.g., honesty is the best policy, or one should always tell the truth, be responsible for one's own actions, it is wrong to steal, it is wrong to cheat, a democratic society is better than a dictatorship society, say no to drugs, always observe safety precautions).

The redefined taxonomy is at odds with Krathwohl's et al. category 4.0 *Organization*--4.1 *Conceptualization of a value* and 4.2 *Organization of a value system*. The second order 3.3 *Commitment* objective (under 3.0 Valuing in Table 4A) indicates expressing a strongly held value or conviction. It is difficult to understand how one can commit to a value (3.3) without first having already conceptualized the value. Conceptualization of a value seems to be out of order. Conceptualization (4.1) should precede 3.3 Commitment to a value.

Conceptualization of a value is defined by Krathwohl et al. as understanding how a value relates to values already held. This seems to be more at concept building or integration as defined in this book. Thus, to avoid confusion, the 4.0 category has been recast into trusting and committing. Thus, conceptualization of a value is rejected in 4.0 as a 4.1 objective. It does not follow the prerequisite to requisite principle of order (Rule 4). Committing is now the 4.2 objective preceded by 4.1 Trusting. See Table 4C: Summary of Taxonomic Rule Violations.

4.1 Trusting

Trusting means a disposition to have confidence in and rely on a value as a guiding principle. Trusting means understanding how a value relates to values already held and integrating it into a broader or more important value principle. It is the merger of two or more values into a stronger value or value complex. When through experience we find something of greater value or good, and it is similar to currently held values, it is assimilated into the value complex. We are all, as we grow and develop, adjusting our values, which in turn, modifies our feelings and thus, our dispositions and demeanor and behavior.

When two or more values are found to be compatible by experience they blend into a common value, a value complex or principle. This integration builds and strengthens the value and belief in the principle. The complex is the consolidation of consistent and often disparate truths drawn from various value principles (e.g., it is wrong to cheat, + tell the truth, + it is wrong to lie, may emerge as a principle for--honesty is the best policy. It is wrong to steal, + be responsible for your own actions, + it is wrong to envy others' property, may emerge as a principle for--respecting other people's property).

Teachers can predispose students to trusting by using probing questions, by challenging their ideas, by having students analyze and qualify their values, by posing conflicting ideas and problems that require the application of values, and critical and reflective thinking.

Categories 4.1 Trusting and 4.2 Committing parallel the cognitive domain category of evaluation in the analysis and qualification objectives. Values and beliefs serve as external criteria for qualifying an analysis.

4.2 Committing.

Committing means a disposition to internalize and adhere to a value as a guiding principle. Commitment means having and expressing a conviction about a certain value or set of values. It is the identification and acceptance of a strongly held value and compliance with it. Consistent compliance with or adherence to a value becomes a *habit of mind*. When a specific occasion arises the habit of mind directs one's behavior. It relates to what is good and right and is reflected in strengthened dispositions of: should/should not, approve/disapprove, would do it/wouldn't do it, will do it/won't do it.

The individual, through experience, has found an outlook about a form, event, value, or practice and is disposed to express that view as a habit of mind (e.g., tells the truth, abhors certain kinds of food, would help a person in need, is respectful toward the American flag, is patriotic, respects authority, does not use drugs).

Teachers facilitate commitment as a predisposition by using questioning and probing techniques to bring out why students think and feel as they do, and by providing learning experiences which engage and cause them to confront and evaluate values and beliefs. See Table 4F: 4.0 Believing.

Table 4F
Believing (Defined)

4.0 Believing. Disposition to trust and commit to a value as a guiding principle.

   4.1 **Trusting**. Disposition to have confidence in and rely on a value as a guiding principle (e.g., express a strongly held conviction when a situation arises, one would: be honest, be courteous, be helpful, be caring, be respectful, be responsible, observe the law, follow democratic principles).

   Applicable test descriptors: trusts, views, relies, values, believes.

   4.2 **Committing**. Disposition to internalize and adhere to a value principle (e.g., assumes ownership of a value when a situation arises, would always say thank you, would persist in doing something until it is right, would observe the rules, would respect the views of others, would not be prejudiced against others, would tell the truth).

   Applicable test descriptors: supports, participates, persists, practices, joins, adheres, complies.

5.0 Behaving.

In the redefined taxonomy, behaving is defined as a disposition to demonstrate and modify a behavior in accord with a value or belief. Behaving means to function, act, or react in a particular way in accord with values and beliefs. To behave is to bear or comport oneself in a particular way. It reflects a habit of mind, a disposition to act with a certain demeanor.

Affectively, it includes: demonstrating--a disposition to act in accord with a value or belief: and modifying--a disposition to adjust or refine one's acts in accord with one's values and beliefs. The behavior is a facet of one's total being. Collectively, these dispositions mirror one's character and outlook on life. Behaving is different from behavior. Behavior includes the composite cognitive, affective, and psychomotor domain of the individual. Behaving, as used here, is a disposition drawn from values and beliefs which are exhibited in one's demeanor and character.

Krathwohl's et al. 5.0 *Characterization by a value or value complex*, and 5.1 *Generalized set* and 5.2 *Characterization* do not meet the taxonomic criteria of Rule 1: Applicability and Rule 2, Totally inclusive and Rule 5, Communicate the intent. Thus, these have been redefined as demonstrating and modifying. See Table 4C: Summary of Taxonomic Rule Violations.

5.1 Demonstrating.

Demonstrating, as defined here, is a disposition to act in accord with a value or belief. One demonstrates one's values and beliefs in one's behavior. One can be characterized as acting in a certain, almost predictable way. It is the application of a strongly held set of dispositions, values, or beliefs in a particular situation. Consistent adherence to certain dispositions, values, and beliefs become habits of mind and is demonstrated in the character of their behavior.

Teachers can predispose students to demonstrating by engaging them in classroom activities and projects. Teachers observe demonstrating dispositions in the ways students conduct themselves in classroom activities and projects, i.e., in doing their assignments, working with others, in their demeanor, and in their attitudes and interests.

5.2 Modifying.

Modifying means a disposition to adjust or refine one's behavior in accord with values and beliefs. It is the changing of an opinion when new information indicates a needed change. It is the emergence of the worth of various values and beliefs to the point where some become dominant and effect a change in one's dispositions of character, and outlook on life.

Teachers can predispose students to modifying by correcting student work and actions, by pointing out errors and misbehaviors, by explaining why it was an error or misbehavior, by demonstrating or modeling the preferred behavior, by providing learning experiences which engage a variety of values and beliefs and by having students evaluate their own behavior. See Table 4G: Behaving.

A summary of the objectives is presented in Table 4H: Redefined Taxonomy of Educational Objectives: Affective Domain.

Table 4G
Behaving (Defined)

5.0 Behaving. Disposition to demonstrate and modify behavior in accord with a value or belief.

   5.1 **Demonstrating.** Disposition to act in accord with a value or belief (e.g., acting in a certain, almost predictable way, solves problems through rational means, has confidence in doing tasks, reprimands someone for violating a rule or law, avoids drugs, studies hard in school to enter college, adheres to a healthful diet, subordinates instant gratification for longer term goals).

   Applicable test descriptors: does, acts, performs, behaves, demonstrates, practices, serves, uses.

   Applicable acts--student is: honest, good, truthful, responsible, trustworthy, caring, sincere, pleasant, mannerly, polite, respectful, reverent, objective, open-minded, studious, hard working, clean, well groomed, athletic, healthy, moral, ethical, patriotic, law abiding, a lady, a gentleman.

   5.2 **Modifying.** Disposition to adjust or refine acts in accord with values and beliefs (e.g., changing an opinion when new information indicates a needed change, incorporating a strengthened value-- stopped smoking, changed one's diet, now exercises regularly, now observes safety precaution, studies more).

   Applicable test descriptors: adjusts, modifies, refines, corrects, alters.

Table 4H
Redefined Taxonomy of Educational Objectives: Affective Domain

---

Dispositions (prevailing tendencies)
1.0   Receiving. Disposition to be aware, willing, and attentive.
  1.1   **Awareness**. Disposition to be conscious of life around one (e.g., being aware of the surrounding environment, perceives different styles of dress, hears different classroom noises, knows the approximate time of day, is conscience of the attitudes of others).
  Applicable test descriptors: senses, sees, listens, perceives, is aware.
  1.2   **Willingness**. Disposition to choose to tolerate and consider certain experiences rather than ignoring or rejecting them (e.g., listen to specific types of music, listens to the views of others without interrupting, open to watching a film, listens to different points of view).
  Applicable test descriptors: offers, watches, listens, tolerates, is willing, chooses, eagerness.
  1.3   **Attentiveness**. Disposition to attend to certain experiences despite distracting stimuli (e.g., pays attention to what is being said, observes a demonstration, concentrates on the lyrics of a song, listens carefully to a poem, is alert to a potential danger).
  Applicable test descriptors: observes, concentrates, attends, is interested, is focused.

2.0   Responding. Disposition to acquiesce, comply with, and assess a response situation.
  2.1   **Acquiescing**. Disposition to accept ideas, actions and responsibilities suggested by others as worthwhile (e.g., sees the need to complete homework assignments, accepts another person's idea, agrees to participate in an activity, allows another person to hold one's hand).
  Applicable test descriptors: acquiesces, accepts, agrees, allows.
  2.2   **Complying**. Disposition to act with little or no prompting (e.g., helps others without prompting, participates in activities, observes classroom rules, follows directions, practices music lessons without prompting, volunteers to do a task).
  Applicable test descriptors: agrees, complies, observes, follows, obeys, conforms, cooperates, volunteers.

Table 4H (Continued)

2.3 **Assessing.** Disposition to appraise one's feelings about a response (e.g., felt uneasy about reading aloud, enjoyed participating in a group activity, wants to do more, is interested in something, enjoyed singing).
Applicable test descriptors: likes/dislikes, wants to/does not want to, enjoys, is interested/uninterested, felt activity was easy/hard, was satisfied/unsatisfied, is sure/unsure, is ambivalent.

3.0 Valuing. Disposition to accept, prefer, and confirm a value.

3.1 **Accepting.** Disposition to endorse a basic value (e.g., agrees sports are worthwhile, endorses healthful lifestyles, endorses democratic principles, rejects violence, accepts peaceful means for settling disputes, endorses truthfulness, opposes deceit).
Applicable test descriptors: accepts, agrees, endorses, selects, rejects, opposes.

3.2 **Preferring.** Disposition to discriminate among alternative values (e.g., when given a choice situation: thinks one should be honest, thinks one should not use drugs, feels one should help other, feels one should not prejudge others, favors a democratic process, chooses nonviolence, supports chastity).
Applicable test descriptors: favors, selects, prefers, supports, chooses, compares, discriminates.

3.3 **Confirming.** Disposition to verify the worth of a value through experience (e.g., after an experience: feels good about helping someone, sees that patience is a virtue, sees that personal relations are better when one respects the others' opinions, finds satisfaction in cooperating with others, sees merit in being courteous).
Applicable test descriptors: verifies, concludes, rationalizes, tests, justifies, supports, validates, confirms, judges, is disposed to should/should not, would/would not.

Table 4H (Continued)

4.0 Believing. Disposition to trust and commit to a value as a guiding principle.

    4.1 **Trusting**. Disposition to have confidence in and rely on a value as a guiding principle (e.g., express a strongly held conviction when a situation arises, one would: be honest, be courteous, be helpful, be caring, be respectful, be responsible, observe the law, follow democratic principles).

    Applicable test descriptors: trusts, views, relies, values, believes.

    4.2 **Committing**. Disposition to internalize and adhere to a value principle (e.g., assumes ownership of a value when a situation arises, would always say thank you, would persist in doing something until it is right, would observe the rules, would respect the views of others, would not be prejudiced against others, would tell the truth).

    Applicable test descriptors: supports, participates, persists, practices, joins, adheres, complies.

5.0 Behaving. Disposition to demonstrate and modify behavior in accord with a value or belief.

    5.1 **Demonstrating.** Disposition to act in accord with a value or belief (e.g., acting in a certain, almost predictable way, solves problems through rational means, has confidence in doing tasks, reprimands someone for violating a rule or law, avoids drugs, studies hard in school to'enter college, adheres to a healthful diet, subordinates instant gratification for longer term goals).

    Applicable test descriptors: does, acts, performs, behaves, demonstrates, practices, serves, uses.

    Applicable acts--student is: honest, good, truthful, responsible, trustworthy, caring, sincere, pleasant, mannerly, polite, respectful, reverent, objective, open-minded, studious, hard working, clean, well groomed, athletic, healthy, moral, ethical, patriotic, law abiding, a lady, a gentleman.

Table 4H (Continued)

5.2 **Modifying**. Disposition to adjust or refine acts in accord with values and beliefs (e.g., changing an opinion when new information indicates a needed change, incorporating a strengthened value, e.g., stopped smoking, changed one's diet, now exercises regularly, now observes safety precaution, studies more).
Applicable test descriptors: adjusts, modifies, refines, corrects, alters.

Summary

Symbolic and prescriptive information/content inputs are posited as social/cultural and religious morals, customs, theologies, and laws which prescribe *what ought to be*. A set of definitions and conditions and criteria for developing a taxonomy is established. The affective domain objectives are critically evaluated as per the taxonomic criteria. A redefined taxonomy is posited which more accurately reflects affective dispositions (prevailing tendencies) and the learning process. Redefinitions are made in lower and higher order objectives to be consistent with the taxonomic criteria. In particular 4.0 *Organization* is replaced by 4.0 Believing, and 5.0 *Characterization* is replaced by 5.0 Behaving. A redefined taxonomy of affective objectives is presented with suggestions for implementing the affective domain in the classroom.

Questions to Consider

1. What are the prescriptive information/content inputs to the affective objectives? Are there other areas that should be included as inputs?
2. Do you agree or disagree with the rule violations listed in Table 4C?
3. As a teacher, how would you implement the affective objectives in the classroom?
4. Do you believe it is important to emphasize affective objectives? Why?
5. What applicable test descriptors would you add to any of the sub-categories of objectives?
6. Select a lesson you teach. What would be the formal, and prescriptive inputs?

7. How does the redefined affective domain reflect the ideas of constructivism?
8. What questions do you have?

References

1. Bloom, Benjamin S., (Ed.), Englehart, Max D., Furst, Edward J., Hill, Walker H., and Krathwohl, David R. 1956. *Taxonomy of educational objectives. The classification of educational goals,. Handbook I: Cognitive domain*. New York: Longmans, Green, Co.
2. Krathwohl, David R., Bloom, Benjamin S., and Masia, Bertram B. 1964. *Taxonomy of educational objectives. The classification of educational goals, Handbook II: Affective domain*. New York: David McKay Co. Inc.

Chapter 5

The Psychomotor Domain: Redefined

Introduction

As the term implies, psycho--is of the mind and motor--is of muscular movement. Purposeful learning involves cognitive abilities and skills and affective dispositions as prerequisites to the development of psychomotor abilities and skills. One must have knowledge of and be disposed to a value to be able to do a task well. There are only limited things you can do with your face, head, hands, arms, legs, feet, and torso. By far, the hands and fingers are the most adaptable and the face is the most expressive. There are limited things you can do with your hands and fingers--grasp things, hold objects, move the fingers to press keys or buttons, make a fist, clasp hands, etc. These are natural abilities. It is what one knows and how one is disposed that directs one's actions to enable such skills as: operating on the brain, using a computer, repairing an automobile, servicing an appliance, making a cabinet, doing a chemistry experiment, designing a product, writing a book, painting a picture, teaching, playing music, etc. Psychomotor learning is not just *hands on* but *minds-on/hands-on* experiential learning. Psychomotor objectives are largely dependent upon cognitive knowledge and affective dispositions. One does not develop psychomotor skills in a vacuum. People develop psychomotor skills in relation to what they know and how they feel, and their values, goals and expectations. Psychomotor learning can be thought of as *procedural knowledge to develop physical abilities and skills*.

Taxonomies of psychomotor domain objectives have received less attention by teachers than the other domains. This may be because teachers of subject matter disciplines (English, math, science, history, etc.) see themselves as primarily *academicians*. This is unfortunate, because one cannot acquire knowledge without involving some physical part of the body, no matter how slight--even seeing, talking or writing. Teachers of the so-called non-academic subjects (art, music, physical education, typing, home economics, industrial education, etc.) have been viewed as more psychomotor oriented and thus, somehow less academic, less worthy. As pointed out, all subjects contain symbolic, prescriptive, descriptive, and

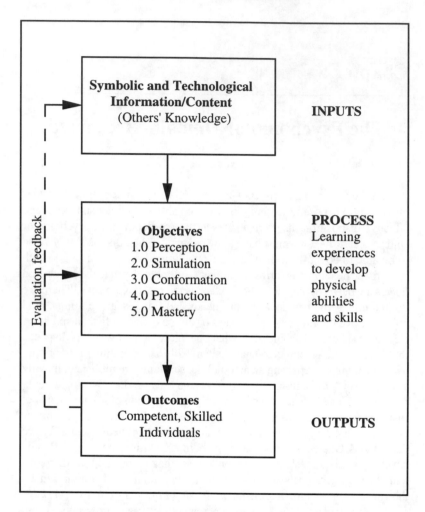

Fig. 5.1 Instructional System for the Psychomotor Domain

Fig. 5.1 shows an instructional system for psychomotor domain with symbolic and technological information/content (others' knowledge) as inputs to the process objectives to develop physical abilities and skills of perception, simulation, conformation, production, and mastery that produce competent, skilled individuals as an output. Evaluation feedback provides for the adjustment of the information/content inputs and process objectives.

technological knowledge.

This book contends that all knowledge (symbolic, prescriptive, descriptive, and technological), and related abilities and skills are worth learning. It is pretentious to select a few subjects and call them *academic*. This is analogous to having a barrel of marbles, representing all of mankind's knowledge, reaching in, taking a handful of marbles, and *saying these are academic* marbles. One marble is no more academic than another. The value and worth of the handful of marbles, or any other handful is determined by the learner, depending on his/her experiences, interests, values, beliefs, goals, and such.

Technological knowledge (knowledge of practice and experience) along with symbolic knowledge are the inputs of emphasis in the psychomotor domain. The process objectives are perception, simulation, conformation, production, and mastery. The output is a competent individual with practical knowledge, abilities and skills, i.e., *know what* and *how to*. See Fig. 5.1 Instructional System for the Psychomotor Domain.

Psychomotor taxonomies to date have focused more on the motor end of the psychomotor continuum as opposed to the median or psycho side. There appeared to be a flurry of psychomotor taxonomy development from 1966 through 1972. Simpson (1966) proposed psychomotor objectives that involve motor skills, the manipulation of materials and objects, and acts that involve neuromuscular coordination. Her seven major categories were: 1) perception, 2) set, 3) guided response, 4) mechanism, 5) complex overt response, 6) adaptation, and 7) origination. Dave (1970) proposed a five-category psychomotor taxonomy to assist in writing objectives. These categories were: 1) imitation, 2) manipulation, 3) precision, 4) articulation, and 5) naturalization. Harrow (1972) set forth a taxonomy of the psychomotor domain. Her categories were: 1) familiarization, 2) fundamentals, 3) development, 4) adjusting and adapting, and 5) perfection and maintenance. In addition, in 1972, Hauenstein proposed a five-category taxonomy of: 1) perceiving, 2) imitating, 3) manipulating, 4) performing, and 5) perfecting. Simpson's, Dave's, Harrow's, and Hauenstein's taxonomies are important for developing psychomotor abilities and skills. However, there has been *no consensus* on what the psychomotor taxonomy should be. There has been a tendency to move away from strictly *motor* to include some *psycho* in the taxonomies. As Herschbach (1975) points out, nearly all psychomotor skills include cognitive as well as affective elements.

For learning and development purposes it seems logical to posit a psychomotor taxonomy that parallels the affective and cognitive domains. Such a taxonomy would provide greater interconnection with the affective and cognitive domains and provide greater utility in applications of the taxonomies. The categories of the psychomotor objectives should be descriptive of the intended level of behavior within the developmental process. Thus, a psychomotor domain with five categories of objectives is posited, which serves to communicate the level of difficulty and development of an individual in the learning process, namely: perception, simulation, conformation, production, and mastery. As in the case of the cognitive and affective domains, each level of the psychomotor taxonomy is dependent upon the preceding level. See Table 5A: Abbreviated Psychomotor Domains: Compared.

Perception, simulation, and conformation are seen as short term objectives. Production and mastery are seen as long term objectives. These require practice and time.

It should be noted again that in psychomotor learning, purposeful development is dependent upon prior cognitive abilities and skills and affective values and beliefs. Thus, requisite information/content must be received (affective domain) and conceptualized (cognitive domain) by an individual before purposeful psychomotor activity can be accomplished. For example, to perceive a task, one must have acquired some general knowledge prior to performing the task. In addition, one typically has some feeling as to the worth or value of the task.

Before proceeding with the discussion of the taxonomy it may be useful to consider some definitions and review the common criteria for structuring a taxonomy.

Definitions

Taxonomy--an orderly classification of things according to their presumed natural relationships, e.g., in classifying abilities and skills, these would be classified according to their difficulty and complexity.

Ability--natural, innate capability, aptitude.

Skill--ability to use one's knowledge effectively and readily in execution or performance, an acquired proficiency. Skill implies a practiced and refined ability.

Taxonomic Criteria/Conditions

A taxonomy is a classification system that establishes the hierarchy of the parts to other parts and parts to the whole. In constructing or evaluating a taxonomy, it is useful to have some common taxonomic criteria and conditions against which the it can be judged. These requisites are listed here as *rules*.

Table 5A
Abbreviated Psychomotor Domains: Compared

Redefined Taxonomy	Various Psychomotor Taxonomies from Literature
Abilities and Skills	
1.0 Perception	**1.00**
1.1 Sensation	Perception, (Simpson, 1966)
1.2 Recognition	Imitation, (Dave, 1970)
1.3 Observation	Familiarization, (Harrow, 1972)
1.4 Predisposition	Perceiving, (Hauenstein, 1972)
2.0 Simulation	**2.00**
2.1 Activation	Set, (Simpson, 1966)
2.2 Imitation	Manipulation, (Dave, 1970)
2.3 Coordination	Fundamentals, (Harrow, 1972)
	Imitating, (Hauenstein, 1972)
3.0 Conformation	**3.00**
3.1 Integration	Guided response, (Simpson, 1966)
3.2 Standardization	Precision, (Dave, 1970)
	Development, (Harrow, 1972)
	Manipulating, (Hauenstein, 1972)
4.0 Production	**4.00**
4.1 Maintenance	Mechanism, (Simpson, 1966)
4.2 Accommodation	Articulation, (Dave, 1970)
	Adjusting and adapting, (Harrow, 1972)
	Performing, (Hauenstein, 1972)
5.0 Mastery	**5.00**
5.1 Origination	Complex overt response, (Simpson, 1966)
5.2 Perfection	Naturalization, (Dave, 1970)
	Perfection & maintenance, (Harrow, 1972)
	Perfecting, (Hauenstein , 1972)
	6.00
	Adaptation, (Simpson, 1966)
	7.00
	Origination, (Simpson, 1966)

Rule 1. The taxonomy must have *applicability,* e.g., be relevant to the function for which it will be used. When the taxonomy is used to classify overt behaviors (abilities and skills) and products of behavior reflecting knowledge, the terms must *be able to expressed* as verbs or gerund nouns (words ending in *ing*). A test for this is, to add *ing* to the terms, thus, perception--perceiving, simulation--simulating, etc.

Rule 2. The taxonomy, as a whole, must be *totally inclusive*--the components represent all categories in a given context, e.g., abilities and skills. The categories must be comprehensive. There should be no error of omission among the parts or between the parts and the whole. As a test, there should be nothing you can think of (any behavior exhibiting an ability or skill) that would not be able to be classified under one of the categories or subcategories.

Rule 3. The categories of the taxonomy must be *mutually exclusive*--there is no overlap between categories or within subcategories of a category. Each category stands independent from the other categories in intent and function. As a test, the subcategories are explicit enough to give definition to the category and the terms used are not repeated within a category. A sub-term in one category can be used in another category. As a principle, it is better not to repeat the term in a category to avoid confusion.

Rule 4. The categories should be arranged following a consistent *principle of order*--e.g., from simple to complex, easy to difficult, concrete to abstract, prerequisite to requisite, etc. If a category is subdivided it must have at least two subcategories which follow the same principle of order.

Rule 5. The *terms* used to identify categories and subcategories should communicate the idea and be representative of those used in the field. A test for this is, *Do the generic terms communicate the intent of objectives to teachers in the field?*

Coding and Process

The major categories may be called first order objectives and can be designated as 1.0, 2.0, 3.0, etc. A subcategory within any first order category may be called a second order objective, e.g., 2.0--2.1, 2.2, 2.3, etc. Further breakdown within an order would be coded with its place and fit within the taxonomy, e.g., 2.--2.1.1, 2.1.2, 2.1.3, etc., 2.2--2.2.1, 2.2.2, 2.2.3, etc.

In developing the second order of objectives, the same Rules 1-5 apply, e.g., 2.0 Simulation, (is now the whole) and any sub-orders established must have applicability, be totally inclusive of simulation, be mutually exclusive to each other, be arranged following a consistent principle of order, and communicate the intent. The same procedure and criteria are used for any third order classification of behavior. The coding, criteria and process would continue ad infinitum.

Redefined Taxonomy of Psychomotor Objectives

The four taxonomies of psychomotor domain objectives from the professional literature are synthesized herein, and portray a process of skill development from initial perception to mastery of the skill(s) or process(es). Each of the categories is presented in turn. For a complete description, see Table 5G: Redefined Taxonomy of Educational Objectives: Psychomotor Domain.

1.0 Perception

To develop a skill requires that one must first perceive the context of an action and what specific actions and abilities are required or involved. The general thrust of 1.00 categories by Simpson (perception), Harrow (familiarization), and Hauenstein (perceiving) appears to be the idea of getting the student aware of the situation.

Perception, as defined here, is the *ability to receive and recognize stimuli in relation to the particulars of concepts, objects, and phenomena.* This implies abilities to receive and conceptualize and sensory readiness.

The redefined taxonomy delineates perception as: 1) sensation, 2) recognition, 3) observation, and 4) predisposition. Simpson's 2.00 *Set* contains the idea of a predisposition. See Table 5B: Perception.

Table 5B
Perception (Redefined)

1.0 Perception. Ability to receive and recognize stimuli in relation to the particulars of concepts, objects, and phenomena. Implies prior abilities to receive and conceptualize and have operative senses.

   1.1 **Sensation**. Ability to sense specific stimuli through one or more of the senses, (e.g., see a shape, hear someone whisper, taste saltiness, feel a piece of grit on a surface, smell an odor in the air).
      Applicable test descriptors: sees, hears, smells, tastes, feels.

   1.2 **Recognition**. Ability to identify and relate specific stimuli and cues with particular concepts, ideas, objects or phenomenon, (e.g., identify a piece that fits into a puzzle by shape and color, taste the tartness as that of a lemon, identify a sound that indicates equipment

---

Table 5B (Continued)

---

malfunction, recognize the odor in the air as fresh-baked bread, feel a texture as abrasive, feel the weight of a glass as half full).

Applicable test descriptors: recognizes, identifies, associates.

1.3   **Observation**. Ability to recognize and associate multiple cues as to the quality or characteristic of a concept, idea, object or phenomena (e.g., recognize and relate the sounds, conditions, and procedures to the safe operation of a table saw, discern the relationships of movements and sounds to dance steps and rhythm, recognize the position of the pencil and direction of strokes and proportions to draw the letters of the alphabet, relate the instruments and procedures to the dissection of an insect).

Applicable test descriptors: observes, recognizes, relates, discerns, views.

1.4   **Predisposition**. Ability to sense, grasp, or discern the general worth or value of a concept, idea, object, or phenomenon, and the inclination to feel or act in a certain way (e.g., watching the teacher draw letters of the alphabet and wanting to try it, sense the value of following a safety precaution, watching a demonstration on the dissection of a frog and having an aversion to doing a dissection, observing a presentation on metrics and feeling neutral, listening to music and wanting to dance).

Applicable test descriptors: acts, reacts, responds, likes, feels, senses.

2.0 Simulation

After a student has perceived a specific situation, the next step is to cause the student to move from a perception to *try out or duplicate* a pattern of specific actions in accord with a general model or situation. This idea is echoed by Simpson's 3.00 (guided response) and the 2.00 categories of Dave (manipulation), Harrow (fundamentals), and Hauenstein (imitating). The idea is to shape or form a degree of dexterity and aptitude.

Simulation means to duplicate in condition, form, nature or character. It is to the *ability to activate, imitate, and coordinate natural abilities to form or shape an act or pattern of behaviors in accord with a general model or situation.* In this case, it is to move from a perception to an action. This implies prior perception, comprehension and willingness to comply or try out a task or an act.

The redefined taxonomy delineates simulation as: 1) activation, 2) imitation, and 3) coordination. See Table 5C: Simulation.

Table 5C
Simulation (Defined)

2.0 Simulation. Ability to activate, imitate, and coordinate natural abilities to form or shape an act or pattern of behaviors in accord with a general model or situation. Implies prior perception, comprehension and willingness to comply or tryout a task or act.

  2.1 **Activation.** Ability to initiate natural actions in accord with a general model (e.g., jump two feet, grasp a tool, lift a weight, swing your arms, touch your toes with legs straight, say *ah*).
Applicable test descriptors: grasps, jumps, holds, lifts, swings, bends, twists, speaks, smiles, pronounces.

  2.2 **Imitation**. Ability to copy or repeat an act or task in accord with a specific model (e.g., light a welding torch and adjust oxygen and acetylene flame to proper color as demonstrated, play piano notes and chords as shown, measure and mix chemicals as demonstrated, get fingers to strike the designated typewriter keys, pronounce pe-riph-ar-sis, round off numbers to the nearest hundred as shown).
Applicable test descriptors: mimics, repeats, imitates, models, copies.

  2.3 **Coordination**. Ability to pattern actions into a controlled order or sequence of movement to a point of suitable aptitude (e.g., do jumping jacks, type a sentence, slice vegetables using the knuckles and fingers of one hand as a moving guide while slicing with a knife with the other hand and coordinating the hand movements into a smooth but rapid pattern to produce slices, load a paintbrush correctly and apply paint with proper brush strokes to artwork, finger and pick guitar strings to make proper notes).
Applicable test descriptors: coordinates actions, tries tasks, patterns movements, acts out, uses implements.

3.0 Conformation

The next step in developing skills is to sufficiently practice the skills to conform to an ascribed standard or criteria. This idea is reflected in the taxonomies of Dave (precision), Harrow (development), and Hauenstein (manipulating).

Conformation, as defined here, means the *ability to integrate aptitudes and perform acts with ascribed qualities and characteristics to the point of skill recognition*. This implies prior valuing, application, and simulation abilities. The redefined taxonomy delineates conformation as: 1) integration, and 2) standardization. See Table 5D: Conformation.

Table 5D
Conformation (Defined)

3.0 Conformation: Ability to integrate aptitudes and perform acts with ascribed qualities and characteristics to the point of skill recognition.

  3.1 **Integration**. Ability to transfer and combine two or more aptitudes into more complex patterns or tasks, (e.g., receive a football hike from the center, back step, read the field, and pass; finger and pick guitar strings in proper sequence and rhythm; insert paper, set margins and tabs, read copy and type a page, and make corrections; boot-up a computer, activate an application, set format and page layout, and keyboard; write a paper in legible cursive using proper grammar, spelling, punctuation).
  Applicable test descriptors: integrates, merges, coordinates, writes, draws, assembles, disassembles.

  3.2 **Standardization.** Ability to perform tasks with ascribed qualities and characteristics to the point of skill recognition (e.g., receive a football hike from the center, back step, read the field, and pass on target within three seconds; finger and pick guitar strings in proper sequence, rhythms and volumes; boot-up, activate application, set format, read copy accurately, type a page within specified time and accuracy limits; draw a 12'-9" x 14'-3" room floor plan using a scale of 1/4" = 1' and proper architectural conventions).
  Applicable test descriptors: conforms, demonstrates, performs, makes, models, adopts.

4.0 Production

The next step in developing skills is to use skills routinely to *produce* a desired act or procedure. The individual can use their skills to perform on a regular, ongoing basis. The skills have become second nature to the individual and the skills and processes can be demonstrated as needed. This idea is somewhat reflected by Dave (articulation), Harrow (adjusting and adapting), and Hauenstein (performing) and by Simpson (5.00 complex overt response).

Production is defined as the *ability to maintain, and accommodate efficient and effective techniques and skills to perform designated functions.* This implies prior believing, evaluation, and conformation abilities and skills.

The redefined taxonomy delineates production as: 1) maintenance, and 2) accommodation. See Table 5E: Production.

Table 5E
Production (Defined)

4.0 Production. Ability to maintain, and accommodate efficient and effective techniques and skills to perform designated functions. Implies prior believing, evaluation and conformation abilities and skills.

   4.1 **Maintenance.** Ability to perform activity routines which yield the prescribed or desired effects or products (e.g., consistently perform a task with the prescribed levels of skill efficiency, quality and character; play a variety of musical arrangements with skill and feeling, act parts in plays, build different kinds of cabinetry according to specifications, use keyboard skills with different formats, use tool skills to disassemble and assemble mechanisms, use measurement skills to make various layouts, use running and jumping skills to play basketball and soccer, prepare a variety of delicious and nutritious meals, use a variety of techniques to produce desired artwork, pilot a commercial airplane, teach a class). *Applicable test descriptors*: produces, practices, performs, operates, works, assembles, builds, dismantles, dissects, fixes, measures, manipulates, maintains.

   4.2 **Accommodation**. Ability to reconcile and infuse changes in skills and processes into ongoing practice (e.g., incorporate a new safety regulation into a current practice; infuse a new dance step routine into a production; edit, reorganize, reformat and rewrite a story; test alternative techniques and methods to determine the most efficient and effective means for the conditions). *Applicable test descriptors*: infuses, reconciles, modifies, adjusts, adapts, accommodates.

5.0 Mastery

The highest level of psychomotor development is stated as mastery. At this level, the individual seeks to become better, to do better, *to excel*, to be able to demonstrate their expertise and artistry. This idea is reflected by Harrow (perfection and maintenance), and Hauenstein (perfecting).

Mastery is defined here as the *ability and desire to originate and perfect abilities and skills. It is the pursuit and refinement of abilities and skills to excel.* This implies prior behaving, synthesis, and production abilities and skills.

Mastery is delineated as: 1) origination, and 2) perfection. See Table 5F: Mastery.

Table 5F
Mastery (Defined)

5.0 Mastery: Ability and desire to originate and perfect abilities and skills. The pursuit and refinement of abilities and skills to excel. Implies prior behaving, synthesis and production abilities and skills.

　5.1　**Origination**. Ability to purposefully or creatively change the composition of the tasks and skills to produce a new technique, process or product, (e.g., develop a new dance step or routine, create a new art technique or form, invent a tool to do a better job, design a new product or structure, develop a new process).
　　　　Applicable test descriptors: creates, innovates, modifies, adjusts, designs, revises, develops.

　5.2　**Perfection.** Ability and desire to seek and achieve higher levels of competence, expertise, wisdom, artistry, and sensitivity, (e.g., to achieve, to be the best you can be, get 100 on the test, make the sports team, graduate with honors, to become: a violin virtuoso, a champion swimmer, a poet, an author, a craftsman, an artisan, a teacher, an astronaut).
　　　　Applicable test descriptors: seeks, pursues, perfects, masters, excels.

The summary of the psychomotor domain objectives is shown in Table 5G: Redefined Taxonomy of Educational Objectives: Psychomotor Domain.

Table 5G
Redefined Taxonomy of Educational Objectives: Psychomotor Domain

---

1.0 Perception. Ability to receive and recognize stimuli in relation to particulars of concepts, ideas, objects, and phenomenon. Implies prior abilities to receive and conceptualize and have operative senses.

1.1 **Sensation**. Ability to sense specific stimuli through one or more of the senses (e.g., see a shape, hear someone whisper, taste saltiness, feel a piece of grit on a surface, smell an odor in the air).
Applicable test descriptors: sees, hears, smells, tastes, feels.

1.2 **Recognition**. Ability to identify and relate specific stimuli and cues with particular concepts, ideas, objects or phenomenon, (e.g., identify a piece that fits into a puzzle by shape and color, taste tartness as that of a lemon, identify a sound that indicates a malfunction in equipment, recognize the odor in the air as fresh-baked bread, feel a texture as abrasive, feel the weight of a glass as half full).
Applicable test descriptors: identifies, associates, detects, recognizes.

1.3 **Observation**. Ability to recognize and associate multiple cues as to the quality or characteristic of a concept, idea, object or phenomena (e.g., recognize and relate the sounds, conditions, and procedures to the safe operation of a table saw, discern the relationships of movements and sounds to dance steps and rhythm, recognize the position of the pencil and direction of strokes and proportions to draw the letters of the alphabet, relate the instruments and procedures to the dissection of an insect).
Applicable test descriptors: recognizes, relates, discerns, views, observes.

1.4 **Predisposition**. Ability to sense, grasp, or discern the general worth or value of a concept, idea, object, phenomenon, and the inclination to feel or act in a certain way (e.g., watching the teacher draw letters of the alphabet and wanting to try it, sense the value of following a safety precaution, watching a demonstration on the dissection of a frog and having an aversion to doing a dissection, observing a presentation on metrics and feeling neutral, listening to music and wanting to dance).
Applicable test descriptors: acts, reacts, responds, likes, feels, wants, senses, inclined.

Table 5G (Continued)

2.0 Simulation. Ability to activate, imitate, and coordinate natural abilities to form or shape an act or pattern of behaviors in accord with a general model or situation. To move from a perception to an action. Implies prior perception, comprehension and willingness to comply or tryout a task or an act.

   2.1   **Activation.** Ability to initiate natural actions in accord with a general model (e.g., jump two feet, grasp a tool, lift a weight, swing your arms, touch your toes with legs straight, say *ah*).
       Applicable test descriptors: grasps, jumps, holds, lifts, swings, bends, twists, speaks, pronounces.

   2.2   **Imitation.** Ability to copy or repeat an act or task in accord with a specific model (e.g., light a welding torch and adjust oxygen and acetylene flame to proper color as demonstrated, play piano notes and chords as shown, measure and mix chemicals as demonstrated, get fingers to strike the designated typewriter keys, pronounce pe-riph-ar-sis, round off numbers to the nearest hundred as shown).
       Applicable test descriptors: mimics, repeats, imitates, models, copies, pronounces.

   2.3   **Coordination**. Ability to pattern actions into a controlled order or sequence of movement to a point of suitable aptitude (e.g., do jumping jacks, type a sentence, slice vegetables using the knuckles and fingers of one hand as a moving guide while slicing with a knife with the other hand and coordinating the hand movements into a smooth but rapid pattern to produce slices, load a brush correctly and apply paint with proper brush strokes to artwork, finger and pick guitar strings to make proper notes.
       Applicable test descriptors: coordinates actions, tries tasks, patterns movements, acts out, uses implements.

3.0 Conformation. Ability to integrate aptitudes and perform acts with ascribed qualities and characteristics to the point of skill recognition. Implies prior valuing, application, and simulation abilities.

Table 5G (Continued)

3.1 **Integration.** Ability to transfer and combine two or more aptitudes into more complex patterns or tasks, (e.g., receive a football hike from the center, back step, read the field, and pass, finger and pick guitar strings in proper sequence and rhythm, insert paper, set margins and tabs, read copy and type a page, and make corrections, boot-up a computer, activate an application, set format and page layout, and keyboard (type), write a paper in legible cursive using proper grammar, spelling, punctuation).
Applicable test descriptors: integrates, merges, coordinates, writes, draws, assembles, disassembles.

3.2 **Standardization.** Ability to perform tasks with ascribed qualities and characteristics to the point of skill recognition (e.g., receive a football hike from the center, back step, read the field, and pass on target within three seconds, finger and pick guitar strings in proper sequence, rhythms and volumes, boot-up, activate application, set format, read copy accurately, type a page within specified time and accuracy limits, draw a 12'-9" x 14'-3" room floor plan using a scale of 1/4" = 1' and proper architectural conventions).
Applicable test descriptors: conforms, demonstrates, performs, makes, models, adopts.

4.0 Production. Ability to maintain, and accommodate efficient and effective techniques and skills to perform designated functions. Implies prior believing, evaluation, and conformation abilities and skills.

4.1 **Maintenance.** Ability to perform activity routines which yield the prescribed or desired effects or products (e.g., play a variety of musical arrangements with skill and feeling, act parts in plays, build different kinds of cabinetry according to specifications, prepare a variety of delicious and nutritious meals, use a variety of techniques to produce desired artwork, pilot a commercial airplane, teach a class).
Applicable test descriptors: produces, practices, performs, operates, works, assembles, builds, dismantles, dissects, fixes, measures, manipulates, maintains.

Table 5G (Continued)

4.2   **Accommodation**. Ability to reconcile and infuse changes in skills and processes into ongoing practice (e.g., incorporate a new safety regulation into a current practice; infuse a new dance step routine into a production, edit, reorganize, reformat and rewrite a story, test alternative techniques and methods to determine the most efficient and effective means for the conditions).
      Applicable test descriptors: infuses, reconciles, modifies, adjusts, adapts, accommodates.

5.0 Mastery. Ability and desire to originate and perfect abilities and skills. The pursuit and refinement of abilities and skills to excel. Implies prior behaving, synthesis, and production abilities and skills.

5.1   **Origination**. Ability to purposefully or creatively change the composition of the tasks and skills to produce a new technique, process or product, (e.g., develop a new dance step or routine, create a new art technique or form, invent a tool to do a better job, design a new product or structure, develop a new process).
      Applicable test descriptors: creates, innovates, modifies, adjusts, designs, revises, develops.

5.2   **Perfection.** Ability and desire to seek and achieve higher levels of competence, expertise, wisdom, artistry, and sensitivity, (e.g., to achieve, to be the best you can be, get 100 on the test, make the sports team, graduate with honors, to become: a violin virtuoso, a champion swimmer, a poet, an author, a craftsman, an artisan, a teacher, an astronaut).
      Applicable test descriptors: seeks, pursues, perfects, masters, excels.

Psychomotor Domain Vector

An initial model of the interrelationships of the cognitive, affective and psychomotor domains was posited by Hauenstein (1972, 22). This model viewed the cognitive domain as a vector with force and magnitude drawn from the subcategories of knowledge, comprehension, application, synthesis, and evaluation. Similarly, the affective domain vector was viewed with force and magnitude drawn from the subcategories of receiving, responding, valuing, organization, and characterization. The cognitive vector was drawn at a right angle to the affective vector. The cognitive and affective forces and

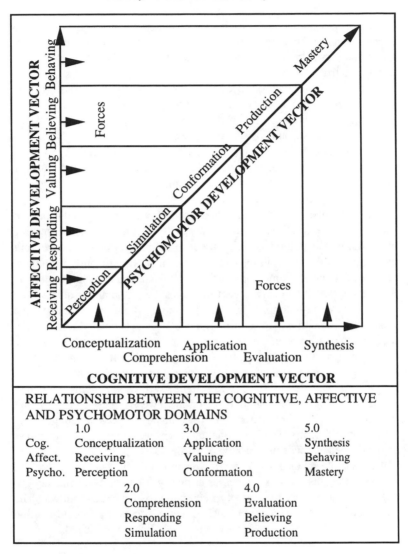

Fig. 5.2 Psychomotor Domain Vector

Fig. 5.2 illustrates the interaction of the cognitive vector (force and magnitude) and an affective vector (force and magnitude) resulting in a psychomotor vector (force and magnitude). In other words, one behaves in accord with the strength of what one knows and the strength of how one feels about it.

magnitudes produced a resultant psychomotor domain vector (drawn at a 45 degree angle). The convergence of the cognitive and affective forces (strengths or weaknesses) is hypothesized to influence the direction and configuration of the psychomotor domain vector. Thus, what one knows, and how one feels, effects what one does. In other words, one acts in accord with what one knows and how one feels about it.

This model has been redefined in terminology to be parallel with the cognitive, affective, and psychomotor domains in this book. Therefore, perception, simulation, conformation, production and mastery replace perceiving, imitating, manipulating, performing and perfecting but, the vector principle and the hypothesis remain the same. See Fig. 5.2 Psychomotor Domain Vector.

As stated, one performs in relation to what one knows about a task or situation and how one feels about it. For example, you may dislike washing a car because it is hard work (you scrub in small circles because your cleaning agent doesn't dissolve the grime) and you are only washing it because it has been six months. On the other hand, you may enjoy washing the car because the new detergent dissolves the grime and requires little work (requires only long, light sweeping motions) and you like driving a clean car. The difference in performance is in what you know (about detergents) and how you feel (motivation and value of a clean car) and the technique used (sweeping rather than scouring motions). If you find the work satisfying you may be inclined to wash the car every week or so.

Fig. 5.3A Detailed in Fig. 5.3 Resultant Psychomotor Domain Vectors shows, how a moderate cognitive vector and a weak affective vector result in a skewed psychomotor vector. The weak affective forces and magnitudes are not of sufficient strength to equal the cognitive and thus, results in less than a desired effect or undesirable performance.

The example in Fig. 5.3B Comparative shows the effects of cognitive and affective strengths and/or weaknesses upon psychomotor performance. For example, students are to conduct a chemistry experiment as follows. The experiment problem/task is: produce Z gas. Students are to confirm that when chemicals A, B, C, and D are combined, Z gas is produced.

Performance check list:
   Read problem correctly
   Selected correct chemicals ABCD
   Measured proportions correctly
   Used proper tools and apparatus
   Followed proper procedures
   Produced Z gas

Student #1 Performance

A: Affective. Disposition for accurateness, carefulness. Is conscientious.

C: Cognitive. Has knowledge of concepts, principles, procedures.

PM: Psychomotor performance: produced Z gas. Applied principles and procedures correctly, read problem/task accurately, selected correct chemicals, measured proportions accurately, used proper tools and procedures.

Is: Satisfied, feels good in achieving.

Student #2 Performance

A: Affective: Weak. Disposed to carelessness, inaccurateness. Is lackadaisical.

C: Cognitive. Strong knowledge of concepts, principles, procedures.

PM: Psychomotor performance: did not produce Z gas. Read task/problem inaccurately, selected correct chemicals, measured proportions inaccurately, used proper tools, followed proper procedures.

Is: Unsatisfied, frustrated, perhaps concerned.

Student #3 Performance

A: Affective: Strong disposition for accurateness, carefulness. Is conscientious.

C: Cognitive. Weak concept, does not know principles, knows general procedure.

PM: Psychomotor performance: did not produce Z gas. Read task/problem accurately, selected correct chemicals, measured proportions accurately, did not use proper tools or follow prescribed procedures.

Is: Unsatisfied, frustrated, concerned.

Affective Domain Vector

When students encounter new information and start to develop some knowledge they also develop some disposition about it. For example, they like it, see that it's useful, feel frustrated, are suspicious, are neutral or indifferent, get excited, get motivated, etc. How they *feel* is in relation to their prior knowledge, values, beliefs, skills, and experiences. It is through learning experiences, through the *doing* that perceptions, preferences, feelings, opinions, values, etc., are strengthened, weakened, modified, altered, developed and changed. Thus, a learning experience becomes critical in that it includes aspects that relate to the affect. It is during the learning experience that feelings, preferences, opinions, values, etc., are

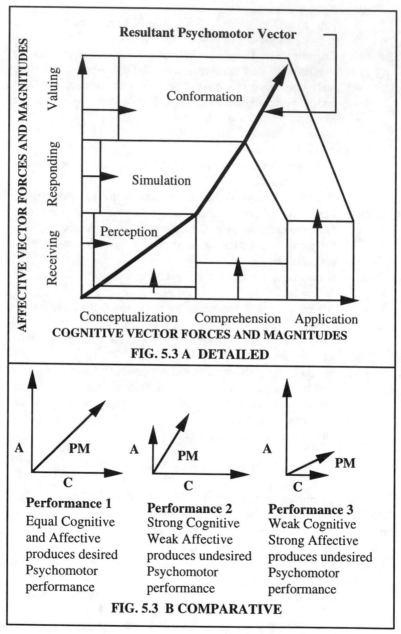

Fig. 5.3 Resultant Psychomotor Domain Vectors

tested for validity and worth. For example, a student who may have an aversion to picking up a frog or a snake, after having handled one, finds that it was not so bad after all. It was OK. In fact, they may feel a small sense of satisfaction or accomplishment in addressing their aversion or fear. The aversion has been weakened by the experience.

Experiential learning is critical in developing the whole individual, particularly the affect. It is through the perception, simulation, and conformation objectives that positive values and dispositions are developed. This requires teachers to do more than just talk or lecture about something. Teachers must carefully structure learning experiences in which students not only acquire knowledge and skills but also provide experiences which help students test their preferences, opinions, feelings, biases, prejudices, etc., and develop their values, morals and beliefs along with their knowledge and skill.

There is seldom a lesson that one cannot find an affective dimension. In mathematics, which is typically thought to be a highly structured discipline, predispositions need to be introduced for accurateness, orderliness, neatness, following the rules and principles, checking for errors and such. In everyday classroom discussions, students need to develop dispositions toward others, e.g., to be respectful of others' views, be cooperative and supportive, be courteous, be open minded, etc., and that they can participate and make worthwhile contributions, and increase their self-esteem and self-concept.

Teachers need to provide the minds-on/hands-on experiences (e.g., simulation and conformation) which enable students to see for themselves how knowledge is applied or used and the validity and worth of the knowledge, what it feels like to use the knowledge, and the assessment of their own abilities and skills. It is through the doing experiences or activities that students discover who they are, what they know and can do, and how well they can perform. The experience adds to their self-concept and self esteem. It is through the experience that values are confirmed or questioned, beliefs are supported or weakened, and dispositions, attitudes, and perceptions are modified. Without active and interactive experiences, little happens other than intellectual speculation and supposition.

The point is, the *affect* disposition is the result of experiences. It is the result of interacting with the world. Thus, on the one hand, teachers can only talk about (theirs or others) values, preferences, attitudes, morals, beliefs, etc., that is, provide a mind set for a student's predisposition. Students, on the other hand, will not fully understand or have a sense of or have ownership of the value until they have had an experience of their own with the worth of the value.

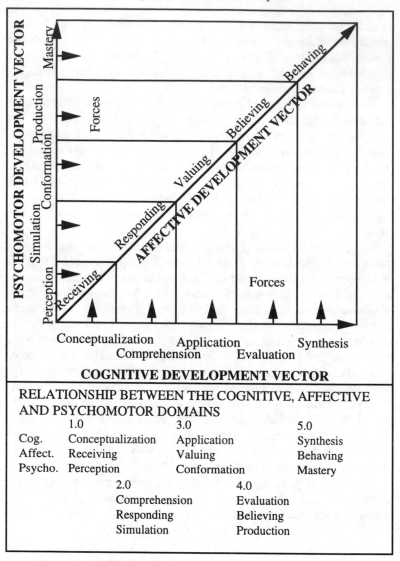

COGNITIVE DEVELOPMENT VECTOR

RELATIONSHIP BETWEEN THE COGNITIVE, AFFECTIVE
AND PSYCHOMOTOR DOMAINS

	1.0	3.0	5.0
Cog.	Conceptualization	Application	Synthesis
Affect.	Receiving	Valuing	Behaving
Psycho.	Perception	Conformation	Mastery
	2.0	4.0	
	Comprehension	Evaluation	
	Responding	Believing	
	Simulation	Production	

Fig. 5.4 Affective Domain Vector

Fig. 5.4 illustrates that an affective vector can be developed by
providing the appropriate cognitive and psychomotor learning
experiences which result in appropriate affective values, beliefs, and
behavior. How one feels is the result of the learning experiences in
relation to what one knows and can do.

Inasmuch as schooling and education is a socialization process, social values, morals, beliefs and such must be experientially taught. Socialization has seldom been purposefully taught, but by and large it has been left to happenstance. It is equally, if not more important, to provide experiences in which students can develop their values and beliefs and morals as it is to teach for knowledge and skill development. Failure to do so contributes to our current social problems, e.g., disrespect for others: stereotyping, racism, discrimination, abuse, rape, etc. and disrespect for others property--vandalism, thefts, robberies, etc., and disrespect for themselves, i.e., cheat, lie, join gangs, dropout, and use drugs.

As described earlier, the cognitive domain vector has its forces and magnitudes and the affective domain has its forces and magnitudes. The convergence of these vectors produce a resultant psychomotor vector with corresponding forces and magnitudes. For purposeful affective experiences, the vectors can be rearranged. The cognitive and psychomotor vectors can be placed at right angles. The product of these forces and magnitudes produce a result in the affective vector. In other words, in the learning environment, how one *feels* is the result of the learning experience in relation to what one knows and can do. See Fig. 5.4 Affective Domain Vector. Thus, teachers can provide learning experiences in which students acquire and develop knowledge and skills as well as experiences that contribute to value, moral and belief development. To educate the whole child requires that all three domains be included in the learning process. To exclude the affective domain objectives is to short change the student. Accumulations of being short changed result in a deficit in positive social development and behavior.

Summary

The psychomotor domain of taxonomies from the professional literature is reviewed and synthesized into a five-category domain to parallel the cognitive and affective domains. The information/content inputs are symbolic and technological knowledge. Terms are defined and taxonomic rules are established as external criteria. The first order categories are posited as: perception (of initial concepts and actions), simulation (moving from perception to action in accord with a model or situation), conformation (skill recognition in relation to standards), production (regular ongoing use of skills and processes) and mastery (seeking higher levels of skill). The influence of the cognitive and affective domains upon the psychomotor domain is examined via a vector model to show that one behaves in accord with what one knows and how one feels about it. Another vector model examined the influence of the cognitive and psychomotor domains upon the affective domain.

Questions to Consider

1. Select a lesson you teach. What would be the symbolic and technological information/content inputs?
2. What is an ability? What is a skill?
3. What does simulation mean? What does conformation mean?
4. How does production differ from conformation?
5. What is the effect of the cognitive and affective vectors on psychomotor behavior?
6. What is the effect of the cognitive and psychomotor vectors on affective behavior?
7. Can you give an example of how the vector diagrams can be applied to a learning situation? Explain.
8. How does the redefined psychomotor domain reflect the ideas of constructivism?
9. What question do you have?

References

1. Dave, R. H., as reported in Robert J. Armstrong, et. al., 1970. *Developing and writing behavioral objectives.* Tucson, Arizona: Innovators Press.
2. Harrow, Anita, 1972. *Taxonomy of the psychomotor domain: A guide for developing behavioral objectives.* New York: David McKay Co.
3. Hauenstein, A. Dean, 1972. *Curriculum planning for behavioral development.* Worthington, Ohio: Charles A. Jones Publishing Co.
4. Simpson, B. J. 1966. *The classification of educational objectives, Psychomotor domain.* Illinois Teacher of Home Economics, vol. X, no. 4.

Chapter 6

The Behavioral Domain: Defined

Introduction

According to Krathwohl et al. (1964, 7-8) modern research on personality and learning raise serious questions about the value of simple distinctions between the cognitive, affective, and psychomotor domains. Krathwohl et al. indicate the basic question posed by modern behavioral science research is whether or not humans ever do thinking without feeling, acting without thinking, etc. It seems very clear that an individual responds as a *total organism* or *whole being* whenever he/she does respond. Teachers and curriculum makers who state objectives tend to make distinctions between problem solving and attitudes, between thinking and feeling, and between acting and thinking and feeling. These distinctions are reflected in attempts to categorize objectives. In addition, the evaluation of the outcomes of learning has involved many different techniques to evaluate thinking, feeling, and acting. Thus, the distinction of categories provides a means for the evaluation of learning, but not necessarily for learning. It may be artificial to set up objectives for one domain without consideration of the influence of the other two domains.

If it is artificial to set up objectives without consideration of all the domains, then a composite domain is needed for classifying and writing objectives, planning lessons, teaching, learning, and measuring outcomes. Although the cognitive, affective and psychomotor domains are useful categories for writing objectives at different levels and for viewing the developmental learning process, it is not realistic to view them in isolation. That is not the way an individual learns. An individual learns as a whole person. While learning, an individual is thinking, feeling, and doing. As a composite this can be called *acting*. This is not to suggest, however, that each domain cannot be the emphasis of learning and measured independently. The three domains should be viewed as a whole. Thus, a composite and integrated fourth domain is posited as a *behavioral* domain.

The complete set of the taxonomic rules is not repeated in this chapter.

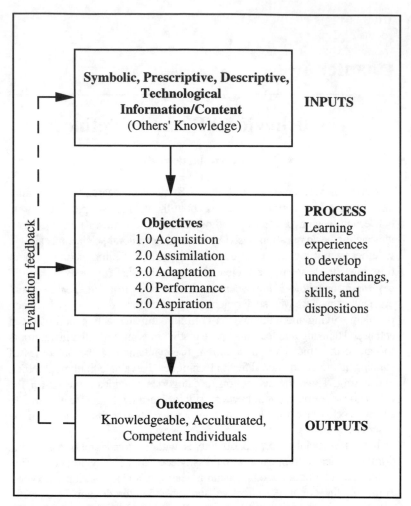

Fig. 6.1 Instructional System for the Behavioral Domain

Fig. 6.1 shows an instructional system for the behavioral domain with symbolic, prescriptive, descriptive, and technological information/content (others' knowledge) as inputs to the process objectives of acquisition, assimilation, adaptation, performance, and aspiration to develop knowledgeable, acculturated, competent individuals as an output. Evaluation feedback provides for the adjustment of the information/content inputs and process objectives.

However, the rules are applied to the new categories of the behavioral domain. These rules are: 1) applicability--be relevant to the function they serve, and be able to be expressed as gerund nouns, 2) be totally inclusive--represent all categories in a given context, 3) be mutually exclusive--no overlap between subcategories or categories and no error of omission, 4) be arranged following a principle of order, and 5) communicate the intent to teachers in the field.

As per the conceptual framework, the behavioral domain has symbolic, prescriptive, descriptive, and technological information/content (others' knowledge) as inputs. The process objectives to develop understandings, skills, and dispositions are posited as a learning and development process of: *acquisition, assimilation, adaptation, performance,* and *aspiration.* The outcome is a knowledgeable, acculturated, competent individual. Evaluation of the outcomes is fed back to the information/content inputs and process objectives for adjustments. See Fig. 6.1 Instructional System for the Behavioral Domain.

Since the behavioral domain is a composite of the cognitive, affective, and psychomotor domains, it needs to be visualized as a holistic entity with interrelated components. The components of the behavioral domain can be visualized as building blocks of a truncated cube. The foundational layer contains more building blocks than the next layer of blocks, and so forth, until the highest level is achieved. Similarly, the time required to develop understandings, skills, and dispositions is greater at the foundational layer because there are many more blocks. The time required to develop higher levels of development is cumulative with each block and layer adding to the time required for learning, development, and achievement. See Fig. 6.2 Components of the Behavioral Domain.

Behavioral Domain Objectives/Levels

The purpose of the behavioral domain objectives is to provide an overall process of learning with five categories or *levels* of development. These levels of learning and development should help teachers and curriculum planners identify the learning level of students in the classroom and assist in teachers in planning lessons to accommodate their students. The behavioral domain provides a condensed framework (of the three separate domains) for identifying learning levels and simplifying the classifying and writing of objectives, lesson planning, teaching, learning, and measurement of outcomes. The delineation of each objective is as follows.

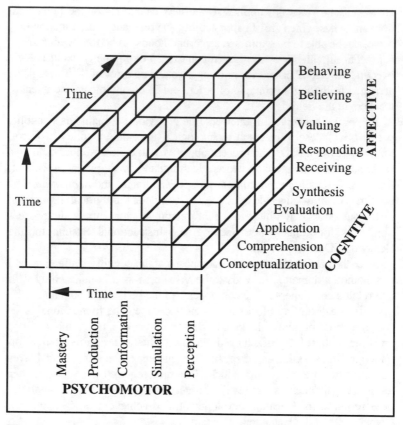

Fig. 6.2. Components of the Behavioral Domain

Fig. 6.2 shows the matrix of building blocks of the behavioral domain. One *behaves* or *acts* in relation to what one *knows*, *feels*, and *can do*. All three domains are essential for each block and level for *whole learning*. The time needed to develop understandings, skills, and dispositions is cumulative. Lower levels require more time because of the number of components. Higher levels require additional time because of the number of layers and block that are prerequisites for attainment.

1.0 Acquisition Objective/Level

Acquisition is defined as the process of receiving, perceiving, and conceptualizing new information/content (a concept or idea) in a specific context. It is generally attentive, passive activity, but with the senses responsive to stimuli and the mind receptive to information. Acquisition includes perceptual association of signs, symbols, and meanings by recognition, recall, identification, observation, and generalization of new information to establish knowledge, and feelings about it.

The purpose of the acquisition objective is to enable students to acquire new concepts, ideas, vocabulary, information, etc., about symbolic, prescriptive, descriptive, and technological understandings, skills, and dispositions.

As a first step, the teacher can present new information/content as directly as possible. The teacher can present the new information/content (inputs) by media, computers, readings, pictures, presentations, and by demonstrations. Students should be able to perceive the context and the ideas. In the process the teacher should define and explain what the concept or idea is, and is not, by exemplars. Teachers can check on the acquisition process by asking students to identify, define, and generalize the specific information presented.

2.0 Assimilation Objective/Level

Assimilation is defined as the process of comprehending and making responses in a learning situation. It includes the ability to transfer and transform concepts, ideas and actions to a similar context or situation, i.e., interpret, translate, and extrapolate information. It involves students forming and shaping their abilities and aptitudes and coordinating acts in accord with a general model as well as exploring and testing the general validity and value of the new knowledge and acts and strengthening their disposition about their efficacy of their knowledge.

The purpose of the assimilation objective is to enable students to comprehend thoroughly, the newly acquired concept or idea, work it into what they already know, and be able to respond by explaining it in their own words or simulating an example of the concept or act.

As a second step, the teacher can expand the concept by having students discuss the idea, ask questions, give examples, and the teacher can correct misconceptions and misinterpretations. The teacher can ask questions to verify what students have seen, read, heard, or observed. The teacher should provide experiential activities which enable students to simulate or test or become familiar with the knowledge and/or skill in a practical situation, orally or in writing or by basic activities which follow a model so students can develop dispositions as to the worthwhileness of their knowledge, abilities, and actions.

3.0 Adaptation Objective/Level

Adaptation is defined as the process of modifying knowledge, skills and dispositions to conform to an ascribed quality, criteria, or standard. It includes the ability to demonstrate intellectual and physical abilities and skills with desired qualities and characteristics to do a task or solve a problem in a practical or simulated context and develop a preference for certain values. The initial developmental activity is dependent upon the same or similar situations, principles, or models in which the knowledge and act were first encountered.

The purpose of the adaptation objective is to enable students to develop a degree of skill or competence in using their knowledge and/or abilities to solve problems in real or simulated situations which are similar or different from the context in which the knowledge, skill, and disposition was first encountered.

Teachers can provide problem situations which enable students to practice and adapt their knowledge and abilities to meet an ascribed quality or character in what they know, feel, and can do. Teachers can set up learning activities which enable the student to practice and work with the knowledge or skill to develop a degree of skill and knowledge through experience and confirm the validity and value of their knowledge and skill.

4.0 Performance Objective/Level

Performance is defined as the process of evaluating situations and being productive. It includes the acts of analyzing, qualifying, evaluating, and integrating knowledge, values and beliefs to act in accord with a situation. The learner has valid knowledge, affective values and beliefs, efficient skills, and effective practices developed to the point of *ownership* and can perform in new and routine situations with satisfaction, confidence, and well being.

The purpose of the performance objective is to enable students to use their knowledge, dispositions, and skills on an ongoing basis. Students should be able to integrate new knowledge, values, dispositions and skills, along with variations, into their current behavior. Teachers should provide learning situations which enable students to practice using their knowledge, skills, and dispositions to increase their proficiency and establish habits of mind and actions.

5.0 Aspiration Objective/Level

Aspiration is defined as the process of synthesizing knowledge and seeking to master skills and demonstrating these in their behavior. It includes values and beliefs which are demonstrated in knowledge, skills, and dispositions to become proficient, to excel, to perfect, to achieve, and to master complex problems or situations. It involves a student's seeking to acquire advanced knowledge of practice, higher level skills, values, expertise, higher levels of sensitivity, artistry, creativity, and wisdom. It is highly persistent and independent activity seeking to apply knowledge, skills, values, and beliefs efficiently, effectively, and creatively. It involves the internalization of knowledge, abilities to perform, and a value and belief system which are reflected in their behavior, character, and lifestyle. The student makes rational judgements and decisions based on their knowledge, practical experience, and values and beliefs.

The purpose of the aspiration objective is to enable students to increase their level of understandings, dispositions, and skills to a higher levels of expertise. Teachers can provide students motivational situations, complex problems, projects, activities, etc., which encourage and challenge students to do better, to be the best, and to incorporate these changes in their values and beliefs into their behavior.

Taxonomy of Behavioral Domain Objectives

The taxonomy of the behavioral domain objectives/levels capsulizes and summarizes the co-requisite objectives of the cognitive, affective, and psychomotor domains. The objectives signify functional levels of intended development and outcomes. These can be applied to any student at their age-grade learning level. The following taxonomy of objectives is self-explanatory. See Table 6A: Taxonomy of Behavioral Domain Objectives/Levels.

Table 6A
Taxonomy of Behavioral Domain Objectives/Levels

1.0 Acquisition. Ability to receive, perceive, and conceptualize a concept, idea, or phenomenon in a specific context. Generally attentive, passive activity but with the senses responsive to stimuli and the mind receptive to information. Perceptual association of signs, symbols, and meanings by recognition, recall, identification, observation, and generalization of new information to establish concepts, understandings, and feelings about it (e.g., listening to a presentation on Ohm's law (E=IR), understanding and enjoying it, observing a demonstration of the principles on how to do a task and finding it meaningful and of interest, watching a presentation on metrics and feeling confused (hopefully not), reading definitions and examples to discern differences and feeling neutral about them).
Applicable test descriptors:
Receiving: Is aware, attentive, receptive, willing, indifferent, neutral, excited, positive, negative, interested, curious.
Conceptualization: Can examine, observe, describe qualities and characteristics; relate a cause to an effect; define qualities, limits, and meaning; generalize in relation to a specific concept, idea, object or phenomenon.
Perception: Can recognize, name or state, spell, pronounce, label, list, match, select, identify, and associate in relation to a specific concept, idea, object, or phenomena.

2.0 Assimilation. Ability to comprehend and make appropriate responses in a situation. Ability to transfer and transform concepts, ideas and perceptions to a similar situation. Students can interpret, translate, and extrapolate information. Can form and shape abilities and aptitudes and coordinate acts in accord with a general model. Ability to explore and test the general validity and value of knowledge and acts in a specific context and strengthen the disposition about their efficacy (e.g., reading homework materials in preparation of doing the assignment, doing math problems using model principles and procedures and finding them valid, discussing the pro's and con's of a certain idea and forming an opinion about it, trying-out or duplicating an action and determining its utility, role playing what it's like to be: blind, praised, rejected, etc.).

Table 6A (Continued)

Applicable test descriptors:

Responding: Is acquiescent, willing, satisfied, predisposed, inclined--
to share, work together, do assignments, observe rules, question.

Comprehension: Can translate, interpret, extrapolate in relation to new
knowledge, convert, defend, distinguish, estimate, explain, extend,
generalize, give examples, infer, paraphrase, rewrite, outline,
summarize.

Simulation: Can copy or duplicate a general model, coordinate
movements, show an aptitude, try-out specific tasks.

3.0 Adaptation. Ability to modify knowledge, skills and dispositions which
conform to ascribed qualities, criteria, and standards. Ability to
demonstrate intellectual and physical abilities and skills with desired
qualities and characteristics to do a task or solve a problem in practical
or simulated contexts and exhibit a preference for certain values. Initial
developmental activity is dependent upon the same or similar situations,
principles, or models in which the knowledge and act were first
encountered, (e.g., applying safety procedures in setting up and using
equipment, using spelling rules to spell new words, doing an
experiment using proper procedures, following procedures to solve
mathematics problems, using principles to assess a situation).

Applicable test descriptors:

Valuing: Is committed to a value or conviction, e.g., being: courteous,
honest, mannerly, friendly, careful, compliant, accurate, cooperative,
fair, helpful, tolerant, patient, responsible.

Application: Can integrate, assimilate and adapt knowledge, abilities
and skills to solve singular problems, demonstrate a task or skill with an
ascribed quality or character.

Conformation: Can write, compute, demonstrate, modify, operate,
predict, produce, show, solve, use, manipulate, demonstrate a task or
skill with an ascribed quality or character.

4.0 Performance. Ability to evaluate situations and be productive. Includes
the act of analyzing, qualifying, evaluating, and integrating knowledge,
values and beliefs to act in accord with the situation. The learner has
valid knowledge, dispositions and values, efficient skills, and effective
practices developed to the point of *ownership* and can function in new

---

Table 6A (Continued)

and routine situations with satisfaction, confidence, and well being (e.g., can read books and relate them, can prepare a variety of in delicious and nutritious meals, can assess and evaluate a situation or problem in accord with criteria, can survey a piece of land, can play tennis, can work with quadratic equations, can dress herself and take care of her own grooming needs). Knowledge, values, skills, habits and abilities are modified through new knowledge of practice by adjusting to fit new or different situations through: accommodating (yielding or giving in a necessary degree or amount), and conforming (bringing an act into accord with a pattern, example, or principle), and reconciling (demonstrating the consistency or congruity of things that seem incompatible). New knowledge and practices are then applied to new or similar situations and more difficult problems (e.g., solving a new problem in accord with the principles of the new example, judging a new situation and testing the validity of concepts, ideas, principles, values, and applications) and adjusting one's general behaviors accordingly.

Applicable test descriptors:

Believing: Has certain values and beliefs. Is reliable, conscientious, responsible, empathetic, loving, open, honest, nonprejudicial.

Evaluation: Can analyze, qualify and evaluate knowledge and values, break down, subdivide, diagram, differentiate, quantify, assess, critique, distinguish, illustrate, infer, outline, separate.

Production: Can operate as a matter of routine, can produce, can accommodate new skills, knowledge and abilities to fit the situation. Can categorize, conclude, explain, modify, summarize, decide, appraise, compare, contrast, evaluate, judge their own and others knowledge, values, beliefs, skills, abilities and acts.

5.0 Aspiration. Ability to synthesize knowledge and seek to master skills and demonstrate these in behavior. Students can synthesize, hypothesize, and resolve complex problems, and seek to originate and perfect their abilities and skills. Values and demonstrates skills to become, to excel, to perfect, to achieve, to master. Seeks to acquire advanced knowledge of practice, higher level skills, values, attitudes, and abilities, higher levels of sensitivity, expertise, artistry, creativity, and wisdom. Highly persistent and independent activity seeking to apply

Table 6A (Continued)

knowledge, skills and abilities efficiently, effectively, and creatively. Internalization of knowledge, abilities to perform, and value system are reflected in behavior, character, and lifestyle. Makes rationale judgements and decisions based on valid knowledge, practical experiences, and values and beliefs (e.g., the learner studies hard and gets 100 on the spelling test, seeks to apply sensitivity to elements in producing artwork, works at perfecting craftsmanship in making objects, edits and rewrites compositions, works at: becoming a champion debater, a mathematician, a teacher.)

Applicable test descriptors:

Behaving: Is determined, inspired, tenacious, independent, disposed to achieve or become, is rational, philosophical, wise.

Synthesis: Can generate, hypothesize, moralize, solve more complex problems, design, rearrange, reconstruct, reorganize, revise, redefine, write, rewrite, plan, create, innovate, invent.

Mastery: Doing better, mastering, excelling, increasing: artistry, sensitivity, expertise, creativity.

Assessment of Behavioral Levels

Individuals engage all three domains collectively in learning, which is reflected in their overall behavior. Again, it is suggested that in any given context, one does not merely *know*, but has some affect about what one knows. One does not merely *do* or perform, but performs in accord with some knowledge and affect. One does not merely *feel*, but feels in relation to their knowledge and experience. One *behaves* or *acts* in relation to what one *knows* and *feels* and *can do*. See Fig. 6.2 Components of the Behavioral Domain.

The composite of the *know*, *feel*, and *do* is one's performance *act* or behavior. If this hypothesis is true, it seems useful then to provide a model of the interrelationships of the three domains and the resultant behavior. The interface of these forces produce a resultant force, or *behavioral* vector.

Due to the complexity in depicting the interrelationships of four dimensions in a three-dimensional world, the cognitive, affective, psychomotor and behavioral vector forces (strengths or weaknesses) can be profiled. Thus, for assessment purposes, a student's level of development or achievement in any of the domains or overall performance can be charted to make a profile of their status at any given time. See Fig. 6.3. Behavioral Profile.

More specifically, on a daily classroom basis, students may be at one of the following levels. See Table 6C: Indicators of Behavioral Levels. These levels should help teachers identify the level of a students' ability and help teachers tailor their lessons in accord with the students' level of knowledge, ability and skills, and dispositions.

Daily of Short Term Objectives

For many teachers and students, learning revolves around the first three objectives/levels: acquisition, assimilation, and adaptation. These are foundational building blocks to higher levels of development and achievement. See Table 6B: Daily or Short Term Objectives.

Table 6B
Daily or Short Term Objectives

1.0 **Acquisition**--the recall of prior knowledge and the willingness to gain new concepts, perceptions and understandings.
2.0 **Assimilation**--the comprehension of information and acquiescence to respond or simulate in accord with a general model or situation.
3.0 **Adaptation**--the application of knowledge to various situations and development of requisite skills with ascribed qualities, characteristics, and values.

Unit or Long Term Objectives

The last two levels are used less frequently because of the amount of accumulated knowledge, skill, and affect necessary to engage them. Performance and Aspiration may be more appropriately exhibited near the end of a unit or a course or after a lengthy period of learning. This is not to say that levels 4.0 Performance and 5.0 Aspiration cannot be introduced intermittently or as desired or necessary. These are shown in Table 6D: Unit or Long Term Objectives.

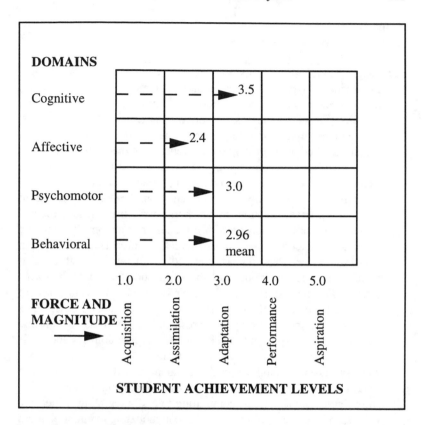

Fig. 6.3 Behavioral Profile

Fig. 6.3 shows that a student's progress in the cognitive, affective, psychomotor and behavioral domain can be represented as a profile of development or achievement. The cognitive, affective, and psychomotor domains can be evaluated independently, or the levels of achievement can be averaged and stated as a mean in the behavioral domain.

Table 6C
Indicators of Behavioral Levels

1.0 Acquisition level. Ability to receive, perceive and conceptualize information to develop understandings. Students are receiving, aware, stimulated, receptive and attentive. They are conceptualizing, perceiving, recalling and observing new knowledge of terms and facts, conventions, trends and sequences, classifications and categories, criteria, methodology, principles and generalizations, and theories and structures. They are observing phenomenon and forming concepts, perceptions, feelings, understandings and predispositions.

2.0 Assimilation level. Ability to transfer and transform understandings to similar or different situations in which they were first encountered and pattern responses in accord with a model or situation. Students are translating, interpreting, and extrapolating information. They can transform perceptions into actions and coordinate their abilities to comply with a general model and find satisfaction (worth) in their acts.

3.0 Adaptation level. Ability to modify their knowledge and acts in accord with the principles, values and criteria in various situations. Students are applying principles and procedures to solve a problem, testing and verifying dispositions and values, and developing abilities and skills with ascribed qualities and characteristics.

4.0 Performance level. Ability to evaluate situations and act in accord with values and beliefs. Students are analyzing, qualifying, and evaluating information and situations, committing to and integrating values and beliefs, and routinely producing and accommodating to minor changes in acts and beliefs.

5.0 Aspiration level. Ability to synthesize knowledge and behave in a manner reflective of values and beliefs. Students are synthesizing, hypothesizing, and resolving complex problems, and seeking to originate and perfect their acts and skills. Students are striving to achieve higher levels of expertise and exhibiting those dispositions, values and beliefs in their behavior.

Writing Objectives.

For the practicing teacher it is difficult, if not confusing, to keep the traditional 63 categories of objectives in mind in planning lessons and writing objectives. It would be useful to the practitioner to focus on five

Table 6D
Unit or Long Term Objectives

4.0 **Performance**--the evaluation of situations and functioning productively in accord with values and beliefs.

5.0 **Aspiration**--the striving to resolve complex problems and achieve higher levels of knowledge, skill, and expertise in accord with values and beliefs.

---

objectives which serve to specify a learning and development process, e.g., acquisition, assimilation, adaptation, performance, and aspiration.

Currently, most objectives are focused on cognitive acquisition of knowledge and comprehension and to a lesser extent, application of that knowledge. This is understandable because of the amount of bits of knowledge that need to be combined for conceptualization and comprehension. The contention here is, that these objectives must be balanced with co-requisite affective and psychomotor objectives (blocks) for complete learning to take place. Seldom is this the case. In particular, it is suggested that receiving, responding and valuing have been shorted, not to mention purposeful perception, simulation and conformation. Without these co-requisites, *whole learning* is incomplete. There is a need to integrate all three domains into the learning process and write objectives which recognize all three aspects.

No attempt is made here to provide information on how to write objectives or measure achievement. There are numerous books in the professional literature on writing objectives for a lesson and measurement thereof. The following example is in the traditional mode of writing objectives to show application to the behavioral domain. For example, at the upper elementary level, and at the *adaptation level*, and in the traditional mode of writing objectives: *After listening to presentations and observing demonstrations on linear metric measurement, measure and record the dimensions of various objects to within plus or minus one millimeter*. The condition or *given* (information input) is *after listening to presentations and observing demonstrations on linear metric measurement*. The cognitive elements are prior conceptualization, comprehension and expression of linear metric measurement. The co-requisite qualitative task is: measure various objects and record dimensions. The assessment criterion is: *to within plus or minus one millimeter*. The prior affective response is a

Table 6E
Abbreviated Taxonomy of Educational Objectives

Behavioral Domain	Cognitive Domain	Affective Domain	Psychomotor Domain
	Short Term Objectives		
1.0 Acquisition Receiving Perception Conceptualization	Conceptualization Identification Definition Generalization	Receiving Awareness Willingness Attentiveness	Perception Sensation Recognition Observation Predisposition
2.0 Assimilation Responding Comprehension Simulation	Comprehension Translation Interpretation Extrapolation	Responding Acquiescing Complying Assessing	Simulation Activation Imitation Coordination
3.0 Adaptation Valuing Application Conformation	Application Clarification Solution	Valuing Accepting Preferring Confirming	Conformation Integration Standardization
			Long Term Objectives
4.0 Performance Believing Evaluation Production	Evaluation Analysis Qualification	Believing Trusting Committing	Production Maintenance Accomodation
5.0 Aspiration Behaving Synthesis Mastery	Synthesis Hypothesis Resolution	Behaving Demonstrating Modifying	Mastery Origination Perfection

disposition for being accurate. The prior psychomotor simulation is the proper placement and reading of the rule and recording the numbers. Teachers who want to write specific objectives as per a selected domain and level should consult the summary of objectives presented in Table 6E: Abbreviated Taxonomy of Educational Objectives. A summary of the applicable test descriptors, as presented in this book, are presented in Appendix C: Applicable Test Descriptors.

Summary

Symbolic, prescriptive, descriptive, and technological information/content are the essential inputs to the learning and development process. The behavioral domain is a composite of the cognitive, affective, and psychomotor domains. It is emphasized that, in a given context, one does not merely *know*, but has some affect about what one knows. One does not merely *do* or perform, but performs in accord with some knowledge and affect. One does not merely *feel* but feels in relation to their knowledge and experience. One *behaves* or acts in relation to what one *knows* and *feels* and *can do*. The composite of the know, feel, and can do is one's performance *act* or *behavior*.

The composite of receiving, conceptualization, and perception is posited as 1.0 Acquisition. The composite of responding, comprehension, and simulation, is posited as 2.0 Assimilation. The composite of valuation, application, and conformation is posited as 3.0 Adaptation. The composite of believing, evaluation, and production is posited as 4.0 Performance. The composite of behaving, synthesis, and mastery is posited as 5.0 Aspiration.

Behavioral assessment indicators are described as *levels of development* and achievement related to acquisition, assimilation, adaptation, performance, and aspiration levels. Assessment of these levels of development and achievement is shown by a behavioral profile.

The original number of categories and subcategories is synthesized from 63 to five categories with 15 subcategories in the behavioral domain. It was pointed out that, on a daily basis, most teachers would be concerned with the three short term objectives of acquisition, assimilation, and adaptation. On a long-term basis, two objectives predominate: performance and aspiration.

It is hoped that teachers, curriculum planners, and teachers to be, will have a better understanding of the learning process, be more cognizant of student learning levels, and be better equipped to provide appropriate curriculum, lessons, and objectives for their students for life in society.

We are what we believe, what we think, and most of all, what we do.

Questions to Consider

1. Why should the cognitive, affective, and psychomotor objectives be combined into one entity?
2. What are the characteristics of the behavioral domain objectives/levels?
3. On what level are of development are the students in your classroom?
4. What level of short term objectives are you currently teaching?
5. What implications does the behavioral domain have for the subject you teach?
6. What implications does the behavioral domain have for your current evaluation of students?
7. From a philosophical perspective, is the conceptual framework behaviorism or constructivism? Why?
8. How does the behavioral domain reflect the ideas of constructivism?
9. What questions do you have?

References

1. Krathwohl, David R., Bloom, Benjamin S., and Masia, Bertram B., 1964. *Taxonomy of educational objectives. The classification of educational goals, Handbook II: Affective domain.* New York: David McKay Co.

APPENDIX A

A Condensed Version of the Cognitive Domain of the Taxonomy of Educational Objectives*

KNOWLEDGE

1.00 KNOWLEDGE

Knowledge, as defined here, involves the recall of specifics and universals, the recall of methods and processes, or the recall of a pattern, structure, or setting. For measurement purposes, the recall situation involves little more than bringing to mind appropriate material. Although some alteration of the material may be required, this is a relatively minor part of the task. The knowledge objectives emphasize most psychological processes of remembering. The process of relating is also involved in that a knowledge test situation requires the organization and reorganization of a problem such that it will furnish the appropriate signals and cues for the information and knowledge the individual possesses. To use an analogy, if one thinks of the mind as a file, the problem of knowledge test situation is that of finding in the problem or task the appropriate signals, cues, and clues which will most effectively bring out whatever knowledge is filed or stored.

1.10 KNOWLEDGE OF SPECIFICS

The recall of specific and isolable bits of information. The emphasis is on symbols with concrete referents. This material, which is at a very low level of abstraction, may be thought of as the elements from which more complex and abstract forms of knowledge are built.

1.11 Knowledge of Terminology.

Knowledge of the referents for specific symbols (verbal and nonverbal). This may include knowledge of the most generally accepted symbol referent, knowledge of a variety of symbols which may be used for a single referent, or knowledge of the referent most appropriate to a given use of a symbol.

To define technical terms by giving their attributes, properties, or relations.
Familiarity with a large number of words in their common range of meanings.[1]

*From TAXONOMY OF EDUCATIONAL OBJECTIVES by David R. Krathwohl, Benjamin S. Bloom and Bertram B. Masia. Copyright © 1964 by Longman. Reprinted by permission of Addison-Wesley Educational Publishers Inc.

1.12 Knowledge of Specific Facts

Knowledge of dates, events, persons, places, etc. This may include very precise and specific information such as the specific date or exact magnitude of a phenomenon. It may also include approximate or relative information such or approximate time period or the general order of magnitude of a phenomenon.

> The recall of major facts about particular cultures.
> The possession of a minimum knowledge about the organism studied in the laboratory.

1.20 KNOWLEDGE OF WAYS AND MEANS OF DEALING WITH SPECIFICS

Knowledge of the ways of organizing, studying, judging, and criticizing. This includes the methods of inquiry, the chronological sequences, and the standards of judgement within a field as well as the patterns of organization through which the areas of the fields themselves are determined and internally organized. This knowledge is at an intermediate level of abstraction between the specific knowledge on the one hand and knowledge of universals on the other. It does not so much demand the activity of the student in using the materials as it does a more passive awareness of their nature.

1.21 Knowledge of Conventions

Knowledge of characteristic ways of treating and presenting ideas and phenomena. For purposes of communication and consistency, workers in a field employ usages, styles, practices, and forms which best suit their purposes and/or which appear to suit best the phenomena with which they deal. It should be recognized that although these forms and conventions are likely to be set up on arbitrary, accidental, or authoritative bases, they are retained because of the general agreement or concurrence of individuals concerned with the subject, phenomena, or problem.

> Familiarity with the forms and conventions of the major types of works; e.g., verse, plays, scientific papers, etc.
> To make pupils conscious of correct form and usage in speech and writing.

1.22 Knowledge of Trends and Sequences

Knowledge of the processes, directions, and movements of phenomena with respect to time.

---

[1] Each subcategory is followed by illustrative educational objectives selected from the literature.

Understanding of the continuity and development of American culture as exemplified in American life.

Knowledge of the basic trends underlying the development of public assistance programs.

1.23 Knowledge of Classifications and Categories

Knowledge of the classes, sets, divisions, and arrangements which are regarded as fundamental for a given subject field, purpose, argument, or problem.

To recognize the area encompassed by various kinds of problems or materials.
Becoming familiar with the range or types of literature.

1.24 Knowledge of Criteria

Knowledge of the criteria by which facts, principles, opinions, and conduct are tested or judged.

Familiarity with criteria for judgements appropriate to the type of work and the purpose for which it is read.
Knowledge of criteria for the evaluation of recreational activities.

1.25 Knowledge of Methodology

Knowledge of the methods of inquiry, techniques, and procedures employed in a particular subject field as well as those employed in investigating particular problems and phenomena. The emphasis here is on the individual's knowledge of the method rather than his ability to use the method.

Knowledge of scientific methods for evaluating health concepts.
The student shall know the methods of attack relevant to the kinds of problems of concern to the social sciences.

1.30 KNOWLEDGE OF THE UNIVERSALS AND ABSTRACTIONS IN A FIELD

Knowledge of the major schemes and patterns by which phenomena and ideas are organized. These are the large structures, theories, and generalizations which dominate a subject field or which are quite generally used in studying phenomena or solving problems. These are at the highest levels of abstraction and complexity.

1.31 Knowledge of Principles and Generalizations

Knowledge of particular abstractions which summarize observations of phenomena. These are the abstractions which are of value in explaining, describing, predicting, or in determining the most appropriate and relevant action or direction to be taken.

Knowledge of the important principles by which our experience with biological phenomena is summarized.

The recall or major generalizations about particular cultures.

1.32 Knowledge of Theories and Structures

Knowledge of the *body* of principles and generalizations together with their interrelations which present a clear, rounded, and systematic view of a complex phenomenon, problem, or field. These are the most abstract formulations, and they can be used to show the interrelation and organization of a great range of specifics.

The recall of major theories about particular cultures.
Knowledge of a relatively complete formulation of the theory of evolution.

INTELLECTUAL ABILITIES AND SKILLS

Abilities and skills refer to organized modes of operation and generalized techniques for dealing with materials and problems. The materials and problems may be of such a nature that little or no specialized and technical information is required. Such information as is required can be assumed to be part of the individual's general fund of knowledge. Other problems may require specialized and technical information at a rather high level such that specific knowledge and skill in dealing with the problem and the materials are required. The abilities and skills objectives emphasize the mental processes of organizing and reorganizing material to achieve a particular purpose. The materials may be given or remembered.

2.00 COMPREHENSION

This represents the lowest level of understanding. It refers to a type of understanding or apprehension such that the individual knows what is being communicated and can make use of the material or idea being communicated without necessarily relating it to other material or seeing its fullest implications.

2.10 TRANSLATION

Comprehension as evidenced by the care and accuracy with which the communication is paraphrased or rendered from one language or form of communication to another. Translation is judged on the basis of faithfulness and accuracy; that is, on the extent to which the material in the original communication is preserved although the form of the communication has been altered.

The ability to understand nonliteral statements (metaphor, symbolism, irony, exaggeration).
Skill in translating mathematical verbal material into symbolic statements and vice versa.

2.20 INTERPRETATION

The explanation or summarization of a communication. Whereas translation involves an objective part-for-part rendering of a communication, interpretation involves reordering, rearrangement, or new view of the material.

The ability to grasp the thought of the work as a whole at any desired level of generality.
The ability to interpret various types of social data.

2.30 EXTRAPOLATION

The extension of trends or tendencies beyond the given data to determine implications, consequences, corollaries, effects, etc., which are in accordance with the conditions described in the original communication.

The ability to deal with the conclusions of a work in terms of the immediate inference made from the explicit statements.
Skill in predicting continuation of trends.

3.00 APPLICATION

The use of abstractions in particular and concrete situations. The abstractions may be in the form of general ideas, rules of procedures, or generalized methods. The abstractions may also be technical principles, ideas, and theories which must be remembered and applied.

Application to the phenomena discussed in one paper of the scientific terms of concepts used in other papers.
The ability to predict the probable effect of a change in a factor on a biological situation previously at equilibrium.

4.00 ANALYSIS

The breakdown of a communication into it constituent elements or parts such that the relative hierarchy of ideas is made clear and/or the relations between the ideas expressed are made explicit. Such analyses are intended to clarify the communication, to indicate how the communication is organized, and the way in which it manages to convey its effects, as well as its basis and arrangement.

4.10 ANALYSIS OF ELEMENTS

Identification of the elements included in a communication.

The ability to recognize unstated assumptions.
Skill in distinguishing facts from hypotheses.

4.20 ANALYSIS OF RELATIONSHIPS

The connections and interactions between elements and parts of a communication.

Ability to check the consistency of hypotheses with given information and assumptions.
Skill in comprehending the interrelationships among the ideas in a passage.

4.30 ANALYSIS OF ORGANIZATIONAL PRINCIPLES

The organization, systematic arrangement, and structure which hold the communication together. This includes the "explicit" as well as "implicit" structure. It includes the bases, necessary arrangement, and mechanics which make the communication a unit.

The ability to recognize form and pattern in literary or artistic works as a means of understanding their meaning.
Ability to recognize the general techniques used in persuasive materials, such as advertising, propaganda, etc.

5.00 SYNTHESIS

The putting together of elements and parts so as to form a whole. This involves the process of working with pieces, parts, elements, etc., and arranging and combining them in such a way as to constitute a pattern or structure not clearly there before.

5.10 PRODUCTION OF A UNIQUE COMMUNICATION

The development of a communication in which the writer or speaker attempts to convey ideas, feelings, and/or experiences to others.

Skill in writing, using an excellent organization of ideas and statements.
Ability to tell a personal experience effectively.

5.20 PRODUCTION OF A PLAN, OR PROPOSED SET OF OPERATIONS

The development of a plan of work or the proposal of a plan of operations. The plan should satisfy requirements of the task which may be given to the student or which he may develop for himself.

Ability to propose ways of testing hypotheses.
Ability to plan a unit of instruction for a particular teaching situation.

5.30 DERIVATION OF A SET OF ABSTRACT RELATIONS

The development of a set of abstract relations either to classify or explain particular data or phenomena, or the deduction of propositions and relations from a set of basic propositions or symbolic representations.

Ability to formulate appropriate hypotheses based upon an analysis of factors involved, and to modify such hypotheses in light of new factors and considerations.
Ability to make mathematical discoveries and generalizations.

6.00 EVALUATION

Judgements about the value of material and methods for given purposes. Quantitative and qualitative judgements about the extent to which material and methods satisfy criteria. Use of a standard of appraisal. The criteria may be those determined by a student or those which are given to him.

6.10 JUDGMENTS IN TERMS OF INTERNAL EVIDENCE

Evaluation of the accuracy of a communication from which such evidence as logical accuracy, consistency, and other internal criteria.

Judging by internal standards, the ability to assess general probability of accuracy in reporting facts from the care given to exactness of statement, documentation, proof, etc.
The ability to indicate logical fallacies in arguments.

6.20 JUDGEMENTS IN TERMS OF EXTERNAL CRITERIA

Evaluation of material with reference to selected or remembered criteria.

The comparison of major theories, generalizations, and facts about particular cultures.
Judging by external standards, the ability to compare a work with the highest known standards in its field--especially with other works of recognized excellence.

APPENDIX B

A Condensed Version of the Affective Domain of the Taxonomy of Educational Objectives*

1.0 RECEIVING (ATTENDING)

At this level we are concerned that the learner be sensitized to the existence of certain phenomena and stimuli; that is, that he be willing to receive or attend to them. This is clearly the first and crucial step if the learner is to be properly oriented to learn what the teacher intends that he will. To indicate that this is the bottom rung of the ladder, however, is not at all to imply that the teacher is starting *de nova*. Because of previous experience (formal or informal), the student brings to each situation a point of view or set which may facilitate or hinder his recognition of the phenomena to which the teacher is trying to sensitize him.

The category of *Receiving* has been divided into three subcategories to indicate three different levels of attending to phenomena. While the division points between the subcategories are arbitrary, the subcategories do represent a continuum. From an extremely passive position or role on the part of the learner, where the sole responsibility for the evocation of the behavior rests with the teacher -- that is, the responsibility rests with him for *capturing* the student's attention -- the continuum extends to a point at which the learner directs his attention, at least at a semiconscious level, toward the preferred stimuli.

1.1 AWARENESS

Awareness is almost a cognitive behavior. But unlike *Knowledge*, the lowest level of the cognitive domain, we are not so much concerned with the memory of, or ability to recall, an item or fact as we are that, given the appropriate opportunity, the learner will, merely be conscious of something--that he take into account a situation, phenomenon, object, or stage of affairs. Like *Knowledge* it does not imply an assessment of the qualities or nature of the stimulus, but unlike *Knowledge* it does not necessarily imply attention. There can be simple awareness without specific discrimination or recognition of the objective characteristics of the object, even though these characteristics must be deemed to have an effect. The individual may not be able to verbalize the aspects of the stimulus which cause the awareness.

Develops awareness of aesthetic factors in dress, furnishings, architecture, city design, good art, and the like.

Develops some consciousness of color, form, arrangement, and design in the objects and structures around him and in descriptive or symbolic representations of people, things, and situations. [1]

1.2   WILLINGNESS TO RECEIVE

In this category we have come a step up the ladder but are still dealing with what appears to be cognitive behavior. At a minimum level, we are here describing the behavior of being willing to tolerate a given stimulus, not to avoid it. Like *Awareness*, it involves a neutrality or suspended judgement toward the stimulus. At this level of the continuum the teacher is not concerned that the student seek it out, nor even, perhaps, that in an environment crowded with many other stimuli the learner will necessarily attend to the stimulus. Rather, at worst, given the opportunity to attend in a field with relatively few competing stimuli, the learner is not actively seeking to avoid it. At best, he is willing to take notice of the phenomenon and give it his attention.

Attends (carefully) when others speak -- in direct conversation, on the telephone, in audiences.

Appreciation (tolerance) of cultural patterns exhibited by individuals from other groups--religious, social, political, economic, national, etc.

Increase in sensitivity to human need and pressing social problems.

1.3   CONTROLLED OR SELECTED ATTENTION

At a somewhat higher level we are concerned with a new phenomenon, the differentiation of a given stimulus into figure and ground at a conscious or perhaps semiconscious level -- the differentiation of aspects of a stimulus which is perceived as clearly marked off from adjacent impressions. The perception is still without tension or assessment, and the student may not know the technical terms or symbols with which to describe it correctly or precisely to others. In some instances it may refer not so much to the selectivity of attention as to the control of attention, so that when certain stimuli are present they will be attended to. There is an element of the learner's controlling the attention here, so that the favored stimulus is selected and attended to despite competing and distracting stimuli.

Listens to music with some discrimination as to its mood and meaning and with some recognition of the contributions of various musical elements and instruments to the total effect.

Acquaints himself with significant current issues in international, political, social, and economic affairs through voluntary reading and discussion.

---

[1] Illustrative objectives selected from the literature follow the description of each subcategory.

Acceptance of responsibility for his own health and for the protection of the health of others.

2.3 SATISFACTION IN RESPONSE

The additional element in the step beyond the *Willingness to respond* level, the consent, the assent to responding, or the voluntary response, is that the behavior is accompanied by a feeling of satisfaction, an emotional response, generally of pleasure, zest, or enjoyment. The location of this category in the hierarchy has given us a great deal of difficulty. Just where in the process of internalization the attachment of an emotional response, kick, or thrill to a behavior occurs has been hard to determine. For that matter there is some uncertainty as to whether the level of internalization at which it occurs may not depend on the particular behavior. We have even questioned whether it should be a category. If our structure is to be a hierarchy, then each category should include the behavior in the next level below it. The emotional component appears gradually through the range of internalization categories. The attempt to specify a given position in the hierarchy as *the* one at which the emotional component is added is doomed to failure.

The category is arbitrarily placed at this point in the hierarchy where it seems to appear most frequently and where it is cited as, or appears to be, an important component of the objectives at this level on the continuum. The category's inclusion at this point serves the pragmatic purpose of reminding us of the presence of the emotional component and its value in the building of affective behaviors. But it should not be thought of as appearing and occurring at this one point in the continuum and thus destroying the hierarchy which we are attempting to build.

Enjoyment of self-expression in music and in arts and crafts as another means of personal enrichment.
Finds pleasure in reading for recreation.
Takes pleasure in conversing with many different kinds of people.

3.0 VALUING

This is the only category head by a term which is in common use in the expression of objectives by teachers. Further, it is employed in the usual sense: that a thing, phenomenon, or behavior has worth. This abstract concept of worth is in part a result of the individual's own valuing or assessment, but it is much more a social product that has been slowly internalized or accepted and has come to be used by the student as his own criterion of worth.

Behavior categorized at this level is sufficiently consistent and stable to have taken on the characteristics of a belief or an attitude. The learner displays this behavior with sufficient consistency in appropriate situations that he comes to be perceived as holding a value. At this level, we are not concerned with the relationships among values but rather with the internalization of a set of specified, ideal, values. Viewed from another standpoint, the objectives classified here are the prime stuff from which the conscience of the individual is developed into active control of behavior.

This category will be found appropriate for many objectives that use the term "attitude" (as well as, of course, "value").

An important element of behavior characterized by *Valuing* is that it is motivated, not by the desire to comply or obey, but by the individual's commitment to an underlying value guiding the behavior.

3.1   ACCEPTANCE OF A VALUE

At this level we are concerned with the ascribing of worth to a phenomenon, behavior, object, etc. The term "belief," which is defined as "the emotional acceptance of a proposition or doctrine upon what one implicitly considers adequate ground" (English and English, 1958, p. 64), describes quite well what may be thought of as the dominant characteristic here. Beliefs have varying degrees of certitude. At this lowest level of *Valuing* we are concerned with the lowest levels of certainty; that is, there is more of a readiness to re-evaluate one's position than at higher levels. It is a position that is somewhat tentative.

One of the distinguishing characteristics of this behavior is consistency of response to the class of objects, phenomena, etc. with which a belief or attitude is identified. It is consistent enough so that the person is perceived by others as holding the belief or value. At the level we are describing here, he is both sufficiently consistent that others can identify the value, and sufficiently committed that he is willing to be so identified.

Continuing desire to develop the ability to speak and write effectively.
Grows in his sense of kinship with human beings of all nations.

3.2   PREFERENCE FOR A VALUE

The provision for this subdivision arose out of a feeling that there were objectives that expressed a level of internalization between the mere acceptance of a value and commitment or conviction in the usual connotation of deep involvement in an area. Behavior at this level implies not just the acceptance of a value to the point of being willing to be identified with it, but the individual is sufficiently committed to the value to pursue it, to seek it out, to want it.

Assumes responsibility for drawing reticent members of a group into conversation.
Deliberately examines a variety of viewpoints on controversial issues with a view to performing opinions about them.
Actively participates in arranging for the showing of contemporary artistic efforts.

3.3   COMMITMENT

Belief at this level involves a high degree of certainty. The ideas of "conviction" and "certainty beyond a shadow of doubt" help to convey further the level of behavior intended. In some instances this may border on faith, in the sense of it being a firm emotional acceptance of a belief upon admittedly nonrational grounds. Loyalty to a position, group, or cause would also be classified here.

The person who displays behavior at this level is clearly perceived as holding the value. He acts to further the thing valued in some way, to extend the possibility of his developing it, to deepen his involvement with it and with the things representing it. He tries to convince others and seeks converts to his cause. There is a tension here which needs to be satisfied; action is the result of an aroused need or drive. There is a real motivation to act out the behavior.

Devotion to those ideas and ideals which are the foundations of democracy.
Faith in the power of reason and in methods of experiment and discussion.

4.0 ORGANIZATION

As the learner successfully internalizes values, he encounters situations for which more than one value is relevant. Thus necessity arises for (a) the organization of the values into a system, (b) the determination of the interrelationships among them, and (c) the establishment of the dominant and persuasive ones. Such a system is built gradually, subject to change as new values are incorporated. This category is intended as the proper classification for objectives which describe the beginnings of the building of a value system. It is subdivided into two levels, since a prerequisite to interrelating is the conceptualization of the value in a form which permits organization. *Conceptualization* forms the first subdivision in the organization process, *Organization of a value system* the second.

While the order of the two subcategories seems appropriate enough with reference to one another, it is not so certain that 4.1 *Conceptualization of a value* is properly placed as the next level above 3.3 *Commitment*. Conceptualization undoubtedly begins at an earlier level for some objectives. Like 2.3 *Satisfaction in response*, it is doubtful that a single completely satisfactory location for this category can be found. Positioning it before 4.2 *Organization of a value system* appropriately indicates a prerequisite of such a system. It also calls attention to a component of affective growth that occurs at least by this point on the continuum but may begin earlier.

4.1 CONCEPTUALIZATION OF A VALUE

In the previous category, 3.0 *Valuing*, we noted that consistency and stability are integral characteristics of the particular value or belief. At this level (4.1) the quality of abstraction or conceptualization is added. This permits the individual to see how the value relates to those he already holds or to new ones that he is coming to hold.

Conceptualization will be abstract, and in this sense it will be symbolic. But the symbols need not be verbal symbols. Whether conceptualization first appears at this point on the affective continuum is a moot point, as noted above.

Attempts to identify the characteristics of an art object which he admires.

Forms judgments as to the responsibility of society for conserving human and material resources.

4.2   ORGANIZATION OF A VALUE SYSTEM

Objectives properly classified here are those which require the learner to bring together a complex of values, possibly disparate values, and to bring these into an ordered relationship with one another. Ideally, the ordered relationship will be one which is harmonious and internally consistent. This is, of course, the goal of such objectives, which seek to have the student formulate a philosophy of life. In actuality, the integration may be something less than entirely harmonious. More likely the relationship is better described as a kind of dynamic equilibrium which is, in part, dependent upon those portions of the environment which are salient at any point in time. In many instances the organization of values may result in their synthesis into a new value or value complex of a higher order.

Weighs alternative social policies and practices against the standards of the public welfare rather than the advantage of specialized and narrow interest groups.

Develops a plan for regulating his rest in accordance with the demands of his activities.

5.0   CHARACTERIZATION BY VALUE OR VALUE COMPLEX

At this level of internalization the values already have a place in the individual's value hierarchy, are organized into some kind of internally consistent system, have controlled the behavior of the individual for a sufficient time that he has adapted to behaving this way; and an evocation of the behavior no longer arouses emotion or affect except when the individual is threatened or challenged.

The individual acts consistently in accordance with the values he has internalized at this level, and our concern is to indicate two things: (a) the generalization of this control to so much of the individual's behavior that he is described and characterized as a person by these pervasive controlling tendencies, and (b) the integration of these beliefs, ideas, and attitudes into a total philosophy or world view. These two aspects constitute the subcategories.

5.1   GENERALIZED SET

The generalized set is that which gives an internal consistency to the system of attitudes and values at any particular moment. It is selective responding at a very high level. It is sometimes spoken of as a determining tendency, an orientation toward phenomena, or a predisposition to act in a certain way. The generalized set is a response to highly generalized phenomena. It is a persistent and consistent response to a family of related situations or objects. It may often be an unconscious set which guides action without conscious forethought. The generalized set may be thought of as closely related to the idea of an attitude cluster, where the commonality is based on behavioral characteristics rather than the subject or object of the attitude. A generalized set is a basic orientation which enables the individual to reduce and order the complex world about him and to act consistently and effectively in it.

Readiness to revise judgments and to change behavior in the light of evidence.

Judges problems and issues in terms of situations, issues, purposes, and consequences involved rather than in terms of fixed, dogmatic percepts or emotionally wishful thinking.

5.2 CHARACTERIZATION

This, the peak of the internalization process, includes those objectives which are broadest with respect both to the phenomena covered and to the range of behavior which they comprise. Thus, here are found those objectives which concern one's view of the universe, one's philosophy of life, one's *Weltanschauung* — a value system having its object the whole of what is known or knowable.

Objectives categorized here are more than generalized sets in the sense that they involve greater inclusiveness and, within the group of attitudes, behaviors, beliefs, or ideas, an emphasis on internal consistency. Though this internal consistency may not always be exhibited behaviorally by the students toward whom the objective is directed, since we are categorizing teacher's objectives, this consistent feature will always be a component of *Characterization* objectives.

As the title of the category implies, these objectives are so encompassing that they tend to characterize the individual almost completely.

Develops for regulation of one's personal and civic life a code of behavior based on ethical principles consistent with democratic ideals.

Develops a consistent philosophy of life.

APPENDIX C

Applicable Test Descriptors

Cognitive Domain: Intellectual Abilities and Skills

1.0 **Conceptualization**. Ability to identify, define, and generalize an idea in a specific context.

    1.1 **Identification**.: identifies, names, states, labels, lists, relates, recognizes.

    1.2 **Definition**: defines, relates, states, matches.

    1.3 **Generalization**: describes, reproduces, outlines, writes, explains, generalizes.

2.0 **Comprehension**. Ability to translate, interpret ideas, and extrapolate content information.

    2.1 **Translation**: converts, translates, draws, diagrams, relates, describes.

    2.2 **Interpretation**: gives examples, paraphrases, explains, interprets, represents, tells.

    2.3 **Extrapolation**: infers, projects, predicts, forecasts, estimates, extrapolates, derives, deduces.

3.0 **Application**. Ability to clarify a problem or situation and use appropriate principles and procedures to solve a specific problem or situation.

    3.1 **Clarification**: identifies, discerns, defines, clarifies, isolates, diagnoses.

    3.2 **Solution**: determines, decides, resolves, solves, shows, produces, uses, experiments.

4.0 **Evaluation**. Ability to analyze and qualify information and data or situations to make a judgement.

    4.1 **Analysis**: analyzes, quantifies, breaks down, separates, determines, identifies causes/effects, distinguishes, selects, diagnoses.

    4.2 **Qualification**: discriminates, compares, discerns, distinguishes, reconciles, juxtaposes, moralizes, rationalizes, qualifies, predicts, concludes, critiques, justifies, deduces.

5.0 **Synthesis**. Ability to hypothesize and resolve complex problems which yield new arrangements or answers.

    5.1 **Hypothesis**: guesses, assumes, projects, hypothesizes, formulates, predicts, rationalizes, reconciles, speculates, prognosticates, theorizes, experiments, investigates.

    5.2 **Resolution**: plans, solves, innovates, creates, invents, prescribes, devises, reconstructs, revises, rewrites, redefines.

Affective Domain: Dispositions (prevailing tendencies)

1.0 **Receiving**. Disposition to be aware, willing, and attentive.

    1.1 **Awareness**: senses, sees, listens, perceives, is aware.

    1.2 **Willingness**: offers, watches, listens, tolerates, is willing, chooses, eagerness.

      1.3 **Attentiveness**: observes, concentrates, attends, is interested, is focused.

2.0   **Responding**. Disposition to acquiesce, comply with, and assess a response situation.

      2.1 **Acquiescing**: acquiesces, accepts, agrees, allows.

      2.2 **Complying**: agrees, complies, observes, follows, obeys, conforms, cooperates, volunteers.

      2.3 **Assessing**: likes/dislikes, wants to/does not want to, enjoys, is interested/uninterested, felt activity was easy/hard, was satisfied/unsatisfied, is sure/unsure, is ambivalent.

3.0   **Valuing**. Disposition to accept, prefer, and confirm a value.

      3.1 **Accepting**: accepts, agrees, endorses, selects, rejects, opposes.

      3.2 **Preferring**: favors, selects, prefers, supports, chooses, compares, discriminates.

      3.3 **Confirming**: verifies, concludes, rationalizes, tests, justifies, supports, validates, confirms, judges, is disposed to should/should not, would/would not.

4.0   **Believing**. Disposition to trust and commit to a value as a guiding principle.

      4.1 **Trusting**: trusts, views, relies, values, believes.

      4.2 **Committing**: supports, participates, persists, practices, joins, adheres, complies.

5.0   **Behaving**. Disposition to demonstrate and modify behavior in accord with a value or belief.

      5.1 **Demonstrating**: does, acts, performs, behaves, demonstrates, practices, serves, uses.

      5.2 **Modifying**: adjusts, modifies, refines, corrects, alters.

      Applicable acts--student is: honest, good, truthful, responsible, trustworthy, caring, sincere, pleasant, mannerly, polite, respectful, reverent, objective, open-minded, studious, hard working, clean, well groomed, athletic, healthy, moral, ethical, patriotic, law abiding, a lady, a gentleman.

Psychomotor Domain: Physical Abilities and Skills

1.0   **Perception**. Ability to receive and recognize stimuli in relation to particulars of concepts, ideas, objects, and phenomenon. Implies prior abilities to receive and conceptualize and have operative senses.

      1.1 **Sensation**: sees, hears, smells, tastes, feels.

      1.2 **Recognition**: identifies, associates, detects, recognizes.

      1.3 **Observation**: recognizes, relates, discerns, views, observes.

      1.4 **Predisposition**: acts, reacts, responds, likes, feels, wants, senses, inclined.

2.0   **Simulation**. Ability to activate, imitate, and coordinate natural abilities to form or shape an act or pattern of behaviors in accord with a general model or situation. To move from a perception to an action. Implies prior perception, comprehension and willingness to comply or tryout a task or an act.

      2.1 **Activation**: grasps, jumps, holds, lifts, swings, bends, twists, speaks, pronounces.

2.2 **Imitation**: mimics, repeats, imitates, models, copies, pronounces.

2.3 **Coordination**: coordinates actions, tries tasks, patterns movements, acts out, uses implements.

3.0 Conformation. Ability to integrate aptitudes and perform acts with ascribed qualities and characteristics to the point of skill recognition. Implies prior valuing, application, and simulation abilities.

3.1 **Integration**: integrates, merges, coordinates, writes, draws, assembles, disassembles.

3.2 **Standardization**: conforms, demonstrates, performs, makes, models, adopts.

4.0 Production. Ability to maintain, and accommodate efficient and effective techniques and skills to perform designated acts. Implies prior believing, evaluation, and conformation abilities and skills.

4.1 **Maintenance**: produces, practices, performs, operates, works, assembles, builds, dismantles, dissects, fixes, measures, manipulates, maintains.

4.2 **Accommodation**: infuses, reconciles, modifies, adjusts, adapts, accommodates.

5.0 Mastery. Ability and desire to originate and perfect abilities and skills. The pursuit and refinement of abilities and skills to excel. Implies prior behaving, synthesis, and production abilities and skills.

5.1 **Origination**: creates, innovates, modifies, adjusts, designs, revises, develops.

5.2 **Perfection**: seeks, pursues, perfects, masters, excels.

Behavioral Domain: Understandings, Skills, and Dispositions

1.0 Acquisition. Ability to receive, perceive, and conceptualize a concept, idea, or phenomenon in a specific context. Generally attentive, passive activity but with the senses responsive to stimuli and the mind receptive to information. Perceptual association of signs, symbols, and meanings by recognition, recall, identification, observation, and generalization of new information to establish concepts, understandings, and feelings about it.

Receiving: Is aware, attentive, receptive, willing, indifferent, neutral, excited, positive, negative, interested, curious.

Conceptualization: Can examine, observe, describe qualities and characteristics; relate a cause to an effect, define qualities, limits, and meaning; generalize in relation to a specific concept, idea, object or phenomenon.

Perception: Can recognize, name or state, spell, pronounce, label, list, match, select, identify, and associate in relation to a specific concept, idea, object, or phenomena.

2.0 Assimilation. Ability to comprehend and make appropriate responses in a situation. Ability to transfer and transform concepts, ideas and perceptions to a similar situation. Students can interpret, translate, and extrapolate information. Can form and shape abilities and aptitudes and coordinate acts in accord with a general model. Ability to explore and test the general validity any value of knowledge and acts in a specific context and strengthen the disposition about their efficacy .

Responding. Is acquiescent, willing, satisfied, predisposed, inclined-- to share, work together, do assignments, observe rules, question.

Comprehension: Can translate, interpret, extrapolate in relation to new knowledge, convert, defend, distinguish, estimate, explain, extend, generalize, give examples, infer, paraphrase, rewrite, outline, summarize.

Simulation: Can copy or duplicate a general model, coordinate movements, show an aptitude, try-out specific tasks.

3.0 **Adaptation**. Ability to modify knowledge, skills and dispositions which conform to ascribed qualities, criteria, and standards. Ability to demonstrate intellectual and physical abilities and skills with desired qualities and characteristics to do a task or solve a problem in practical or simulated contexts and exhibit a preference for certain values. Initial developmental activity is dependent upon the same or similar situations, principles, or models in which the knowledge and act were first encountered.

Valuing. Is committed to a value or conviction, e.g., being: courteous, honest, mannerly, friendly, careful, compliant, accurate, cooperative, fair, helpful, tolerant, respectful, patient, responsible.

Application: Can integrate, assimilate and adapt knowledge, abilities and skills, to solve singular problems, do a task, demonstrate a task or skill with an ascribed quality and character.

Conformation: Can write, compute, demonstrate, modify, operate, predict, produce, show, solve, use, manipulate, demonstrate a task or skill with an ascribed quality or character.

4.0 **Performance**. Ability to evaluate situations and be productive. Includes the act of analyzing, qualifying, evaluating, and integrating knowledge, values and beliefs to act in accord with the situation. The learner has valid knowledge, dispositions and values, efficient skills, and effective practices developed to the point of *ownership* and can function in new and routine situations with satisfaction, confidence, and well being.

Believing: Has certain values and beliefs. Is reliable, conscientious, responsible, empathetic, loving, open, honest, nonprejudicial.

Evaluation: Can analyze, qualify and evaluate knowledge and values, break down, subdivide, diagram, differentiate, quantify, assess, critique, distinguish, illustrate, infer, outline, separate.

Production: Can operate as a matter of routine, can produce, can accommodate new skills, knowledge and abilities to fit the situation. Can categorize, conclude, explain, modify, summarize, decide, appraise, compare, contrast, evaluate, judge their own and others' knowledge, values, beliefs, skills, abilities and acts.

5.0 **Aspiration**. Ability to synthesize knowledge and seek to master skills and demonstrate these in behavior. Students can synthesize, hypothesize and resolve complex problems, and seek to originate and perfect their abilities and skills. Values and demonstrates skills to become, to excel, to perfect, to achieve, to master. Seeks to acquire advanced knowledge of practice, higher level skills, values, attitudes, and abilities, higher levels of sensitivity, expertise, artistry, creativity, and wisdom. Highly persistent and independent activity seeking to apply knowledge, skills and abilities efficiently, effectively, and creatively. Internalization of knowledge, abilities to perform, and value system are reflected in behavior, character, and lifestyle. Makes rationale judgements and decisions based on valid knowledge, practical experiences, and values and beliefs.

Behaving: Is determined, inspired, tenacious, independent, disposed to achieve or become, is rational, philosophical, wise.

Synthesis: Can generate, hypothesize, moralize, solve more complex problems, design, rearrange, reconstruct, reorganize, revise, redefine, write, rewrite, plan, create, innovate, invent.

Mastery: Doing better, mastering, excelling, increasing: artistry, sensitivity, expertise, creativity.

INDEX